READING QUEER:
POETRY IN A TIME OF CHAOS

READING QUEER:
POETRY IN A TIME OF CHAOS

Edited by Maureen Seaton and Neil de la Flor

Anhinga Press
Tallahassee, Florida 2018

Cover Image: photograph, "Waiting for the Ballet," by Neil de la Flor
Design, production: C.L. Knight
Type Styles: text set in Minion Pro; authors and titles set in Museo

Library of Congress Cataloging-in-Publication Data

Reading Queer: Poetry in a Time of Chaos — First Edition
ISBN — 978-1-934695-52-4
Library of Congress Cataloging Card Number — 2017947224

Anhinga Press Inc. is a nonprofit corporation dedicated wholly to the publication and appreciation of fine poetry and other literary genres.

For personal orders, catalogs, and information, write to:

ANHINGA PRESS
P.O. Box 3665 • Tallahassee, Florida 32315
Website: www.anhingapress.org • Email: info@anhingapress.org

Published in the United States by Anhinga Press
Tallahassee, Florida • First Edition, 2018

Our labor has become
more important
than our silence.
— Audre Lorde

CONTENTS

INTRODUCTION xv

AARON SMITH
Census (Jon) 1
from Beautiful People in Dramatic Situations 2

BRYAN BORLAND
The Dead and the Married 6
Weather, This 7
The Kitchen Table Treaty 8
The Duane Effect 10
Thunder Road on Martin Street 11

CARIDAD MORO-GRONLIER
What the White Girl Asked at Our 20th High School Reunion 13
When You Go Home with the Fat Chick 14
At Least I Didn't Rape You 16
Cuban-American Lexicon 18

CATHLEEN CHAMBLESS
[Gay Edge Revenge] 19
Alienation 20
Sugarcoated 22

CELESTE GAINEY
rush 501 28
more/less 29
in the days of early polyester 30
in our nation's capital 31
between takes 33

CHERYL CLARKE
Coterie 34
#All this for changing a lane 36

CHING-IN CHEN
[as a space to occupy] crossing the source 37
hunting ancestors 40
a lit ghost 41
various various 42

cin salach
Bi Sexual 44
Why we wander 45
Now. 48

(COBALT) THALO KERSEY
I Tattooed Jesus 49

COLLIN KELLEY
Girl Detective 51
Revenant 52

EDUARDO C. CORRAL
Ceremonial 53
Guillotine 55
Sentence 57

ELIZABETH BRADFIELD
Dispatch from This Summer 58
Learning to Swim 60
Regarding the Absent Heat of Your Skin
on Letters I Receive While at Sea 61
Neko Harbor 63

ELLEN BASS
Taking Off the Front of the House 64
God and the G-Spot 66
The Small Country 67
Ode to Repetition 68

FARAH MILAGROS YAMINI
Thirteen Ways of Looking at an Ass 69
Speaking Between My Soul and Sexy Parts 72

GEM BLACKTHORN
Dissociative Sexuality Disorder 74

GERRY GOMEZ PEARLBERG
OCTO9 75

GREGG SHAPIRO
How To Flirt 80
Dedicated Driver 82
My Mother's Vanity 84

HOLLY IGLESIAS
Reliquary 87
Word Bank 88
The Game of Crones 89
Angelus Novus 90

JAMES ALLEN HALL
The Saw 91
Stock Character 93
Irregular Plurals 94
An American Porn Star Contemplates the Divine 96
Stock Character 98

JAN BECKER
Summer at Jesus Camp (for Donna) 100

JASON SCHNEIDERMAN
The Buffy Sestina 102
Pornography II: The Capacity to Love 104
Pornography IV 105

JEN BENKA
Begin 106
For Muriel 108

JERICHO BROWN
A.D. 113
Layover 114
To Be Asked for a Kiss 116

JIM ELLEDGE
Zigzag adv. [<Ger. *zacke,* a tooth, sharp prong, or point] 121
Umpire vt. [<M.Fr. *nomper,* a third person] 122
Hubbub n. [<Celt. *ubub,* exclamation of aversion] 123
Burlesque adj. [<It. *burlesco <buria,* a jest, mockery] 124
Algebra n. [<Ar. *al-jabr,* the reunion of broken parts] 125

JOSÉ A. VILLAR-PORTELA
a dolphin dies 126
A Life in Heels 131

JOSEPH O. LEGASPI
Revelation 133
Whom You Love 135
Rouge 137

JP HOWARD
A Love Letter to The Decades I have Kissed or Notes on Turning 50 139
149th Street, Sugar Hill, Harlem 141
MARK it UP 142
i am 143
A Leo Love Letter to Myself 144

JULIE MARIE WADE
After Words 145
Shooting Pool with Anne Heche the Day After Ellen & Portia's Wedding 147
Portrait of Tolerance as a Picket Fence 149
Self-Portrait in Ugly Pants 151

JULIE R. ENSZER
Pervert 153
At the New York Marriage Bureau 156
Connubial Hour 157

JUSTIN TORRES
In Praise of Latin Night at the Queer Club 158

KEVIN SIMMONDS
Toll 161
Sermon 163
Salvation 164
Apparition 165

L. LAMAR WILSON
I Can't Help It 167
Resurrection Sunday 168

LORI ANDERSON
Hayley Mills 173
Family-Style 174
Brooklyn American 175

MEGAN VOLPERT
to the tune of "Rosalita" (Springsteen 1973) 176

MEREDITH CAMEL
*Sexual Evolution** 178
My To-Do List 181
Tiptreeing around the Cosmos in Drag 182

NICHOLAS WONG
Airland 183
Intergenerational 184
When the light no longer illuminates, illustrates, or is ill, or I 186
I Imagine My Father Asking Me What Being ______ Is Like, While I Swipe My American Express to Pay for His Lungs' Virus I Don't Know How to Pronounce 188

PHILLIP B. WILLIAMS
Do-rag 190
Eleggua and Eshu Ain't the Same 192

QWO-LI DRISKILL
Loving Day 194
Praise Song to Stone: For My Father 197
Book of Memory 201
Map of the Americas 203

RUBEN QUESADA
Lament 206
I said, Goodbye 207
Two Lovers 208

sam sax
Will 209
Risk 211
Objectophile 212
Surveillance 213

SAMIYA BASHIR
Methods of heat transfer 214
Second law 215
First law 217

SAMUEL ACE
An ocean-like hush 220
Rain a river 225
I have ridden into spring 226

SETH PENNINGTON
Some Birthday 227
Letterman Jacket 230
Skinburst 232

SETH PENNINGTON & BRYAN BORLAND
Abandon 231

SHANE ALLISON
Busch Gardens Photo 233
Sleepless 234

STACEY WAITE
Deadlocked 236
Reading Queer 238

STEPHANIE LANE SUTTON
Ode to Femme 239
When I Think of You I See 240

STEPHEN S. MILLS
Inside the Outside 241
The Act of Vanishing 243
My Parents Talk of Sparrows 245
Pondering Whiteface in Chinese Cinema While Rereading Frank O'Hara's "In the Movies" 247

TARA BURKE
Good and Holy 249
The Blueberry Syrup 251

tc tolbert
Word Problems 254
dear Melissa — 261

VALERIE WETLAUFER
Solitary Vice 262
Insomnia with Solomon 263
One day I laid down the bruise of you 265
Pastoral 266

CONTRIBUTORS' NOTES 269

ACKNOWLEDGMENTS 279

ABOUT THE EDITORS 285

INTRODUCTION

If you are free, you are not predictable and you are not controllable.
—June Jordan

Welcome, reader!

When we began to search for the contents of this anthology at the end of 2015, we did not expect to collect roadmaps. We knew the work would be crucial, even radical. We saw it connecting beautifully with the work in other queer anthologies to showcase and empower our extraordinary community and to widen audiences. We had been invited by the new directors of Anhinga Press in Tallahassee to bring a few dozen queer writers together, and we were, quite simply, delighted by the possibilities.

The work arrived all through winter and spring of 2016 — primarily poetry, with some short prose as well — and it was gorgeous. All of it. Vulnerable, sexy, heartbreaking, revolutionary. Poetry that pushed against and beyond boundaries in both form and content.

> *Queer art can be art that is experimental, complicated, anti-patriarchal; not who the author is doing, but what the text is doing … The queerness is the potential to create beyond what is allowed, be as weird as one wants to be, and fly your freak flag.*
> *— José Villar-Portela*

Then, on June 12, 2016, the unthinkable happened, and 49 people celebrating Pride were killed (and 53 injured) at Pulse in Orlando. When the U.S. presidential election rolled around that November, the world as we knew it ended.

Rereading the submissions after the election, we realized that the work of our fifty poets had become more than crucial, more than powerful. It had become sacred.

(Personal note from Maureen): I don't think I have ever felt as grateful for poetry (and poets!) as I did the month I consumed these words of my queer fellows and sisters after the election. I believe they contributed to saving my life and quite possibly the lives of many of my students as well, with whom I spent increased time through November in the lifeboat of poetry. For the abiding strength, courage, humor, light, and creativity manifested in this volume, I humbly thank our contributors.

(Personal note from Neil): I'm grateful for the all of the voices represented in this anthology, but I'm also keenly (and queerly) aware of the voices we weren't able to include because of space and time constraints. It's those voices, those gaps and silences, that keep me up at night. The Trump Era reminds us once again that access to more queer spaces is not a luxury, but a necessity to foster and preserve our precious culture.

Reading Queer: Poetry in a Time of Chaos brings fifty poets together in the spirit and solidarity of poetry at its finest and fiercest. It is our gift to all conscious citizens. With love.

— Neil de la Flor & Maureen Seaton

READING QUEER:
POETRY IN A TIME OF CHAOS

Aaron Smith

Census (Jon)

In a city of four million cocks,
yours.

Aaron Smith

from Beautiful People in Dramatic Situations

1. Colin Farrell in *In Bruges*

He shot a little boy, so now he wants to kill
himself. Fur-coat
eyebrows, cock-ready

lips. His eyes the kind of black
you stumble in.

2. Julianne Moore in *A Single Man*

How can she know her friend wants to die?
She's planning a party and putting on makeup.

If she cries, the colors on her eyes
will melt perfectly.

3. Tom Hardy in *Locke*

He's trying to do the right thing, a man
in a car with a speaker phone.

I hope his wife leaves him for cheating,
that he never makes it home.

He'll be more beautiful
if he ends up alone.

4. Colin Firth in *A Single Man*

Beige chair, beige phone, brown
sweater, big black glasses
he folds with one hand
before he drops them. Tear

from left eye to lip, tear from right eye
down cheek. If only his dead boyfriend
could lick his face

before he runs to his friend's house
in the rain.

Bryan Borland

The Dead and the Married

Some say our marriage is assimilation,
that you and I are both sides of gentrification:
the old neighborhood and the moving truck. They
think we're dirty boys scrubbed too clean
by bridal showers. Yet my body still politicks,
speaks up as we leave your brother's high school
graduation in our harshest clothes, that stag of a smile
running through the fields of your handsome face.
You pull me through the place you grew
hair and a pair of horns. You know this town,
all carnival bark and shadow story,
the overgrown alleys, the boarded-up windows,
the busted ways to be alive. You drive
to a cemetery, park on the bones of those dead
dreams and we fuck in the dust with the same
swagger that dances in your brother's graduating eyes.
Afterwards, we join the family party,
your shirt untucked, my belt missing, rings
on our fingers that hold the light and the dark.

Bryan Borland

Weather, This

Dear Bryan the storm is soon
to begin I write not in warning as you
will appreciate the autumn flowers
you always wanted The herb garden fragrant
basil and rosemary you think dead from drought
will come alive again in September
Instead I write to bolt down your bones
scarecrow they turn out to be You already know
the direction of these winds The strange
chill of a home in the beginning of wane
A week from now you will be tucked into bed
by a lover who will stab you in your sleep
You will swim in bloody pools
He will tell you dreams and poems mean nothing

Listen dream this poem
How this rain will grow you
a family How some part of you
remembers the hunger of time smells
the blood sees your prints in the mud We are
powerless to what is by right of nature ours
these lunar pulls these campfires warm you night-
bathed when you'll swim together two
untamable things in the breathing river Your arms
will fold like paper birds around him Your histories
will circle starving beasts soon to eat You'll make
shelter of every crater and scar Every pain
a guide Everything is instinct

Bryan Borland

The Kitchen Table Treaty

If this is meant to survive
we must agree now on the terms
of war   itself a contradiction as
war by definition tramples lines

Do not say tonight there will be
no war   you know armies
gather in all backyards   everything
we read can turn against us   the poison
ivy you cut from the fence weeks ago
remains in skeleton vines to crawl again

We have to have these conversations
we are not the enemy   never
with words as weapons across
the table   instead we map the battle
inward   days when one or both of us
carries the madness of the other
like a wounded soldier slung across the back

And believe me now   there will be madness
when we have promised to end these bodies looking
lived in   so at times our breaths
will smell of the adolescent
dank and semen
the swamps we wade through
when absence makes us not ourselves

You are not yourself
today   so I am not myself
but tonight we again will be
ourselves   this is

the treaty of attraction
blood from the wrist of marriage
we are human countries   you and I
the rules of war between us this:
let's just hold
each other tonight ok?
All night.
No sleep.
Okay.

Bryan Borland

The Duane Effect

I buy purple shoes. Duane says
they go with nothing so they go with everything.
The right and the left are different sizes. Duane
talks the clerk into giving me a discount.
At the next store I buy a turquoise
jacket. Duane says it's mint. He tells me
he makes shopping more economical
by swapping price tags from cheaper pieces.
He's developed a technique. Which means
someone someday will pay more for less. I tell him
I worry he'll be punched in the face by a stranger.
He responds by asking a stranger if she likes
to dance. The stranger likes to dance. Duane looks
back at me as if this will save him. It probably will.
Duane lives with a gay couple. I avoid
more shopping by stealing their shirts.
Duane is this type of influence. He tells me
to take one shirt but I take two. I feel like
Duane will appreciate this. I've never met
his roommates. They're traveling when we visit.
My husband and I sleep in their bed. My husband
is my husband because of Duane. Duane sent us
into marriage to queer it from the inside. My husband
and I fuck in Duane's roommates' bed. I press
the underwear I find in the room to my
husband's face. I don't know whose they are.
We use their lube, too. We do not use their edible body paint.
We cum in their towels and pet their dog. We score free
whiskey at the Eagle by wearing stolen jock straps.
Duane is this type of influence. He rents a locker
to house our pants for a quarter.
I keep the purple shoes on.
Duane is right. They go with everything.

Bryan Borland

Thunder Road on Martin Street

Sweetheart. The screen door slams.
There is so much more to say. It's been raining
for five days and everywhere I look are
wedding bouquets. We keep creating
a life together, spending all our extra
income on books and paintings and photographs
of everything we want to love. You write
me poems from the rearranged words
of worn-out Springsteen songs. Your mother
shows me pictures of you as a child I pocket
and tape to our walls. You tell me to throw away
your high school graduation gown. I let it lie
in rags at your feet just to pick it up again.
See, it's the history of you I have to feel.
Sweetheart. The book is finished. The book
of us coming together and already it seems
written by someone I was yesterday. I keep
remembering the things I should have said.
Like how the first gift you gave me was a guitar
off your back, and the way I tried to learn how
to make it talk but my fingers weren't made
for such automatic prayer. Or the afternoon
you proposed in San Francisco with
the camellia glen, or getting high and
walking the Chelsea High Line tightrope
with donuts on our breaths. Sweetheart.
This poem could go on and on.
Like we go on and on.
There will be more poems and more books
and I'll dream your name at night in the street.
I'll try to write about other people and right
my stupid wrongs, but I'll end up saying how
I've held on to you as the map of everything

better. How I touch your chest and your navel
as you sink into things that ease you:
the muscle of literature, a reclaiming
of film, music to sleep to. To wake up
kissing to. How I suppose we've made it
over the sickness after the honey-
moon. The days becoming normal
until we realized they're so not. And suppose
from here on out I promise to write
about anything but you —

— I would fail.
I'm no hero. I'm just the man you married
who sings along to Springsteen songs
and pictures you in every one.

Caridad Moro-Gronlier

What the White Girl Asked at Our 20th High School Reunion

Why weren't we friends in school?

We weren't friends because I knew you
hung out in the American parking lot
unlike my boyfriend who parked his Stingray
in the Cuban one on the other side of school. Of course,
I hung out there. Not that you would understand
why being his girl meant I couldn't
sit in your car at lunch and listen
to your Def Leppard, your Motley Crue,
leave him to fend for himself.

We weren't friends because he courted me
old school, couched beside my father
every Sunday while I served apprentice
to my mother, her eyes onion stung,
arms spattered with marrow and lard,
who played at loving her place at the stove.
Rules I had not yet learned how to break.

We weren't friends because I envied
the way you weren't allowed to settle,
how you were allowed to date assorted breeds
of boys who strutted across the lawn to ring your bell.
Your dad waved his blessing out the door
and didn't worry because he taught you to discern,
to choose among them, to drive yourself,
headlights set on more than the slam
of the same car door, even if it was a Corvette.

Caridad Moro-Gronlier

When You Go Home with the Fat Chick

don't assume
she'll roll over
for something easy
like a Moolatta
from the D.Q.
such an obvious
Coolatta rip-off
Dunkin' Donuts
really should sue
their soft-serve ass
not that you'll
find her there either
she takes her donuts
home with her
unless she's feeling
pleased with herself
then she just might
lick her fingers
and grin
with every bite of
sugar shine on her lips
and though at first
you think you'd prefer
she keep her appetite
under wraps
you realize
there's something
beautiful about
her abandon
the way she takes
her pleasure
'cuz she ain't afraid

to get what she needs,
and she can see
where you are
coming from
versus where
you say you're at
cuz, yea, you'll tell
your crew about
the cushion
you've been pushin'
how the big girl pleaded
for some of your
King Kong love
but deep down
you'll know
it was you
who needed
a bite of something
good to get you
through the night.

Caridad Moro-Gronlier

At Least I Didn't Rape You

The wine we shared did it. You leaned in
and offered me some killer advice

because we both turned to look at the brunette
who passed our table on the way to the bathroom—

Since you're into chicks, you might as well
think as if you had a dick.

You have the power of preemptive strike.
Just follow her into the john,

wait until she leaves the stall, then push her
against the wall. Take what you want.

Most guys won't admit it, but
if we had our way we'd knock you down,

spread your legs and plunge
ourselves into what we want.

I consoled myself with all that could have been worse
than discovering you were the kind of man

my father would have loved, the kind
of man who considered a woman nothing

more than split and cleft, orifice, cavity,
study in absence, a maw, a void;

worse than my girlhood, litany of less than
my father hammered into me

the worst of his words exhumed, corroborated
by the pick and spade of your confession,

Hija, a key that opens many lock is a master key;
don't be the slut with the busted deadbolt.

I'd rather kill you,
than let you become a whore.

At least I didn't rape you.
Don't you know how lucky you are?

Caridad Moro-Gronlier

Cuban-American Lexicon

The word
for girlfriend
in Español
is novia
(Hyphen)
Sweetheart
fiancé
bride.

I was
trained
to be
neither
girl nor
friend
to the boy
I chose
no fun
just duty
down
the aisle
toward
the altar
where
I went
from
novia
to wife
or esposa
(Hyphen)
shackle
manacle
handcuff.

Cathleen Chambless

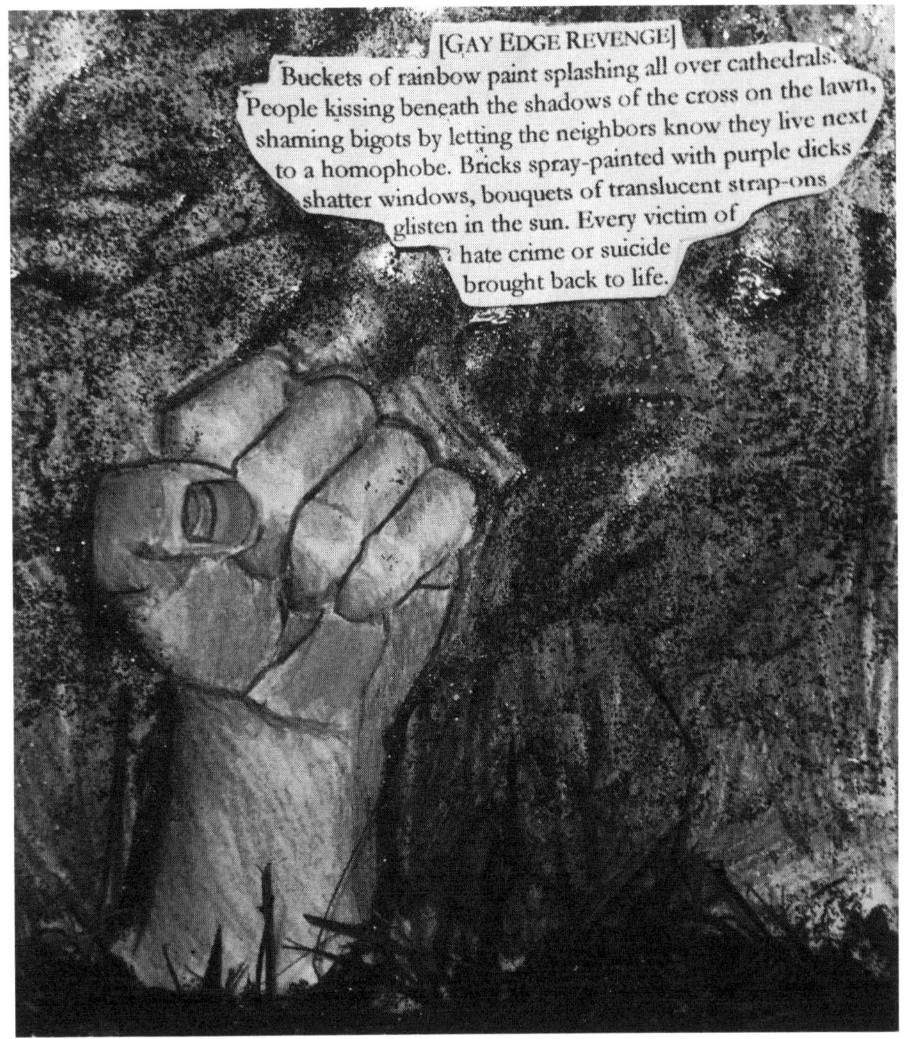
[GAY EDGE REVENGE]
Buckets of rainbow paint splashing all over cathedrals.
People kissing beneath the shadows of the cross on the lawn,
shaming bigots by letting the neighbors know they live next
to a homophobe. Bricks spray-painted with purple dicks
shatter windows, bouquets of translucent strap-ons
glisten in the sun. Every victim of
hate crime or suicide
brought back to life.

Cathleen Chambless

Alienation

Outside of Fox's,
it's 2-4-1 Tuesdays
& I'm 6 whiskey sours
deep as the gravel sludges
under my boots,
& I am suddenly aware
indeed, the Earth does
rotate on its axis
at 1,037 miles per hour,
pretty blue marble
whirling her skirt of clouds.
So, that's why Mars
is always blushing.
Veronica's scarlet
hair collects the blue
light & I want to kiss
her but she's kissing
Victor & everyone
is wearing the same
black shirt & the same
black pants & the same
black boots & the same tattoos
& our similarities
sicken me.
How can I know everyone here,
but feel so alone?
So I walk away.
The streetlamps
are bright & daunting
as they tower over me,
judging me. I stick my middle finger
to them & their Big Brother light bulbs.
I pull my hoodie over my head

& pull my ink out of my purse
& tag KAT on the garbage dump
& alley walls,
& fall over tagging the curb.
Oh, we are animals
with a painter's pallet
of only slightly more sophisticated
forms of territorial pissings.
Mine being ink,
while the alpha has the atom bomb.
BT's flashes in neon pink
& I hope maybe
strippers will make me less lonely,
that one of them will tell me her real name,
kiss me & give me her phone number,
that she won't disappear when I run out of singles,
that I am different than the men
who pay for sex,
because I am a womyn,
because I have an ego,
because I am an animal.
Every animal in the kingdom
will kill to keep their mate their property,
only we kill in the name of morality.
Cheers to
another glass of Walker on the rocks
& Raven's pierced pussy
in my face, wagging
in tune *To the Windows*
To the Walls,
cheers
to the fact that
I
am
so
exquisitely
empty.

Cathleen Chambless

Sugarcoated

Pecha Kucha named after punk songs

[Pink Flower]
Dew drops
fuchsia flesh petals unfold
wrinkled hood, third eye.

[Shaved Pussy Poetry]
If she would learn to speak vagina, she would hear her organ
weep & plead with pink razor blades,
but pleading useless, because all razors are sociopaths.
Stubble & skin snag between metal teeth,
bloody bubbles run down legs,
soon-after hairs burrow beneath pores
with pillows of pus above,
her pussy too sore to make love.

[Alien She]
Orange neck noosed with pearls
pink acrylic shields suffocate
her flimsy, yellow nails.
16 Jell-O shots, 6 used condoms,
& 7 recitations of the Greek alphabet
for admittance. College loans
spent on sisterhood & silicone.

[Rebel Girl]
Granny smith apple eyes & crust locks in her hair–
when she sings she vomits
a wildebeest. Punched a preacher on campus
calling students *Satan's sluts.*
Crying together when we heard
Kathleen Hanna's spoken word.
"Rebel girl, you are the queen of my world."

[Blind Eyes Blind Lives]
Fraternity brothers fill red cups with Natty Ice & ping-
pong balls. Housewives pop valium & read *Cosmopolitan.*
It's American to spend Sunday cheering for
Christ & a football.
It's American to torture & rape:
slut-shame + mini-skirt + *hearsay*=
open & shut case.

[Jigsaw Youth]
amps spew sound waves like bile,
wimmin in neon green, yellow & pink balaclavas
stomp their combat boots & affix with the circle pit,
splashing flashes of rainbow into the
whirlpool of ligaments, tattoo strewn. We don't give a fuck
about what you think you know–
we know
this is dancing.

[Plastic Dream]
Saline, silicone, collagen, augmentation,
liposuction, Botox, blood-laden bandages.
Lubricated tubes slurp blubber,
bloated bags grow microbes beneath breasts.
The doctor says "One procedure left!
You are almost a pretty, pretty, princess!"
Anesthetic overdose leaves her comatose.
Swollen Sleeping Beauty,
a crown of stitches & gauze.

[Diet Pill]
amphetamine chic
red heart star burst coffin hearse
skinny smiling corpse

[The Lies They Want Us to Swallow]
Jesus Christ doesn't like dick lickers — only the heterosexual kind.
Jesus Christ doesn't like wimmin's rights — he took a shit in Mary's mouth.
Jesus Christ doesn't like Medicare — in fact he charged the blind.
Jesus Christ doesn't like environmentalists — he killed the last unicorn
& breathes CFCs.
Jesus Christ doesn't like civil rights — he shot Harvey Milk & Martin Luther King.
Jesus Christ was American, straight & white.

[Legislative Bodies Legislating Bodies]
A Christian pharmacist denies Plan B legally & sells OCs,
two states penetrate patients with plastic probes
to transfer the fetus to a TV screen, while politicians on Fox
debate the definition of "legitimate" rape.
One day the Right Wing will slit stomachs
with an envelope
opener & ignite iron brands,
a uterus sizzles sleek cursive vapor,
the surgeon presses the organ until the burn reads
"Government property."

[The Gift of Life]
arm-pit microchip
suicide prevention nets
whistle while you work

[WRONG BATHROOM]
Plastic stick figures designate doors
to lady or man, silently circumscribing
a red circle & slash over trans. Raped
against a urinal, white teeth cracked
against white tile, a lion limp, fur
saturated in slick crimson.
The poacher pisses on his prey, grins.

[GAY EDGE REVENGE]
Buckets of rainbow paint splashing all over cathedrals.
People kissing beneath the shadows of the cross on the lawn,
shaming bigots by letting the neighbors know they live next
to a homophobe. Bricks spray-painted with purple dicks
shatter windows, bouquets of translucent strap-ons
glisten in the sun. Every victim of
hate crime or suicide
brought back to life.

[BLUE BY DAY, WHITE BY NIGHT]
Miranda Rights void
Fire! suspicious lollipop
Klu Klux Klan in blue

[NO JUSTICE, NO PEACE]
Nazis or
Officers of the USA?
Just doing our duty to
Uphold the law.
Star spangled swastikas killed
Treyvon Martin,
Israel Hernandez & made Garner whisper, *I*

Cant breathe. Who held Holtzclaw's
Erections up their sleeve?
Not his victims, but the state.
Oh say can you see why we are sick of
Pleading? Hearts are
Exploding like
All of the Molotov
Cocktails, their flames vexed &
Etching *No Justice No Peace.*

[Right Wing Warfare]
winged bibles glide
crucifix atomic tick
Christ claps mushroom clouds

[Armageddon Won't Be Brought By Gods,
But By Men Who Think They Are]
Slaughterhouses announce, *Wolves are environmental terrorists.*
The black blood of white wolves pools, red ravines deplete
the snow, as factory farms gush phosphorus & feces into the streams. Oil rigs
in the Gulf explode, sludge funnels into a dolphin's blowhole,
a convenient excuse to send more troops to nuke,
people reduced to decorative busts of intestines & ligaments, while patriotic
parades take place in the States. Fireworks & radiated baby floats
glow, blood spritzes from trumpets every quarter note.

[In the Name of Convenience]
robotic udders
conveyor belt feces meat
No. 5 with Cheese

[Modern Day F*Word]

Feminism,
You are my Samauri sword.
In your defense, I would
commit Seppuku,
slice my stomach agape
let my slick pink
entwinement of entrails
slap on concrete, then write
your name with my blood.

[We Will Continue to Break Your Laws & Destroy Property Until We Win][1]

Sedate the security guards, let them slumber far away. Open
the locks of the Slaughterhouse, set the wild horses free
before they become glue or meat, savor the echo
of whinnies wafting & hooves thudding against the dew-ridden
grass blades. Watch chickens champion as they expand
their wings, feathered dragons silhouette against the rising sun.
Ignite the factory & face the flames as they
lavish the building, lovers having make-up sex.
Now dance.

1 Song Titles by Witch Hunt (Sugarcoated; Blind Eyes Blind Lives; Plastic Dream; Legislative Bodies Legislating Bodies). Daisy Chainsaw (Pink Flower). Huggy Bear (Shaved Pussy Poetry). Bikini Kill (Alien She; Rebel Girl; Jigsaw Youth). Contravene (The Lies They Want Us to Swallow; Blue By Day, White By Night; The Gift of Life; In the Name of Convenience). Tribe 8 (Wrong Bathroom). L7 (Diet Pill). Gayrilla Biscuits (Gay Edge Revenge). Aus Rotten (Right-wing Warfare, No Justice No Peace) Anti-Product (Modern Day F*Word). Appalachian Terror Unit (Armageddon Won't be Brought by Gods, But by Men Who Think They Are; We Will Continue to Break Your Laws & Destroy Your Property Until We Win)

Celeste Gainey

rush 501

I remember buying my first pair
on St. Mark's Place in '71

in some vintage clothing store
you had to walk up stairs to enter,

Joe Cocker—or maybe Leon Russell
blasting on the outdoor speakers.

The Holy Grail: 501s, brass button fly,
washed-out watercolor blue,

worn corners on the right hip pocket
where a wallet had been carried,

a slight cumulus cleft to the left
of the crotch, where he had stashed his bulge.

Putting them on was weird, a crazy rush;
like trying on the groove of a missing person,

something right and wrong at the same time—
an instant sex change operation.

I wore my 501s home on the 747,
with rough-out cowboy boots, poor-boy T-shirt,

midnight blue velvet blazer with wide lapels.
My mother took one look, knew something was up;

saw the groove of a missing person,
something wrong but right at the same time.

more/less

more gay
than queer
more queer
than lesbian
less lesbian
than girl
more girl
than woman
less woman
than man
more boy
than bi
less bi
than butch
more butch
than dyke
more dyke
than trans
less trans
than faggot
more fag
than bulldagger
more bulldagger
than top
less top
than bottom
least top
no top
more bottom
less 's'
more 'm'
more bottom
more bottom
less homo
more sexual

Celeste Gainey

in the days of early polyester

you don't know yet you are flammable;
jars of Miracle Whip, tubs of Polly-O in the fridge.
Your moral imperative on ice, the vertical blinds rattling shut,
sleek sofa of solid kerosene resisting your body's impression.
You keep saying, *Cotton, cotton, the touch, the feel of cotton,*
but you are drawn to the slinky boy shirt with the Kandinsky-like
print, fancy your stubbled side-burns whiskering
the top of its Byronesque collar—long points gesturing toward
no-tits torso, slim hips, bell-bottomed legs, Frye boots.
It feels like Velveeta against your skin, something you might
scrape off with the blade of your Swiss Army knife.
It seems to reject you. Still, you can't stop
parading your shirt through Washington Square Park
in the hot afternoon sun—looking for combustion.

Celeste Gainey

in our nation's capital

on the occasion of viewing the AIDS Memorial Quilt
October 1992, Washington, DC

You motion for me to come sit on your lap.
You carry me to the bedroom.

Undress me. Lay me down
on crisp hotel sheets—

a soft quilt for mothering
in a place where there is no mothering

—only monuments to neglect & regret
where we tread the grassy mall

the length & breadth of
Silence = Death.

No soft breast to suck
as I do yours now:

you are above me pressing
/grinding down on my cunt.

You pull your tit away
turn me over/

lift my buttocks
spread my cheeks.

Then your warm spit
/your tongue rimming me.

I’m on my knees now
rocking hard to your rhythm.

This is church;
the mother-fucking/big-ass

National Cathedral in the dead of night;
black-mass candles blazing,

dead saints watching, mute
& unblinking, from their pedestals,

hollowed eyes of marble politicians
peeping through the stained glass.

You the butch high priestess of too much sorrow
/me the submissive penitent

longing to feel your pain—take it.
Pull it deep inside.

We’re not supposed to be here
/doggie-style in our nation’s capital,

the quilt tending away now,
undulating bodies in retreat—

your aching fist
an anchor at the bottom of me.

Celeste Gainey

between takes

Taxi Driver (1976, Martin Scorsese, dir.)
Columbus Circle, summer 1975

De Niro idles in his Checker. Cybill flirts behind
her Jackie-Os. Scorsese sucks oxygen from a tiny
tank trailed by an assistant. Albert Brooks hogs
the PA: *When using the moving sidewalk,*
please stand to the right, if you wish to pass, please
do so on the left. Over & over. Grips lay dolly track
for a shot we all know will never make the final cut
but will take most of the day to shoot.
Me in my 501s & Mighty Mouse T-shirt,
20 feet up, work gloves & pliers protruding,
the brute arc light I tend sputters & hisses
beside me. Like that famous *New Yorker* cover
showing the world as seen from 9th avenue—
the land of make believe rises up
to swallow me whole.
I try to lean as if belonging against
the unsteady rungs of my ladder—oblivious
to the real world down there too—
passing me by; most, jaded New Yorkers,
their eyes on the prize, but maybe some
looking up & wondering *what's that girl doing*
up there in the sky—flying so close to the sun?
Some kind of myth. With pliers.

Cheryl Clarke

Coterie

Foregrounding foresisters
A different assignment/consignment
to Harper's Ferry or some other then-wooded
place where bloods mix unseen hybrids among conqistadores
and no orthodoxy to speak of
                                        origins
                                        uncertain
marauders
                                        maroons
                                        (muskogee)
and driven as the desert
                                        I
                                        do
                                        want

                                        us

                                        to
                                        understand
a lost syntax
a hostile signifier
the bovine plains

'lucid interval[s]'*

Resist totalizing
essentializing
and truth.
Provisional queerness
no formalist gestures
narcissistic privates made publics
these poetries

these ingroup associations
a coterie of signifieds
systematic chance.
Whose,
oh, my strong reader?

*Borrowed from world-class poet, Ed Roberson's 1984 *Lucid Interval as Integral Music.*

Cheryl Clarke

#All this for changing a lane

(I don't EVEN want to be m.c.-ing another elegy here or rappin out these death similes or samplin these tried and tired tropes, or spittin these beat rhythms, rhymes, and repetitions.)

a fly black Chi-town girl brown skin and open brown face was anything but bland — even in that mug shot and orange jumpsuit: on her way to life by way of Prairie View, Tx. (now joining the long list the *most* infamous) where un-armed black death thrives in cop custody if you're changing lanes and smoking a cigarette at the same time but check it out: you're a fly black Chi-town girl, brown skin and open brown face — even when 'irritated' — smoking a cigarette, being told by a smokey to dump your smoke, bragging 'I will light you up' and dragging you from your car — sorta like lynching, except Sandy was in custody, though not convinced of its lawfulness. Black people get lynched over cigars, cigarettes, cigarillos, whistling, loud music, loud talk, back talk, praying, running, defective tail lights, toy guns, hoodies, and their own wallets. (Mamie Till knew all about lynching. She crowbarred Emmet's casket open, and after spying the tell-tale signet ring, touched every part of what was left of 'little man's' bloated body dredged up from Money, Mississippi.) Don't be black, coming from Chicago, and traveling South, you won't stand the storm, if you are a sassy black teenager or a fly black girl, brown skin and open brown face smoking a cigarette, changing lanes and unused to taking low to nonsense — even fatal nonsense. Better to stay with the extreme temperatures of your Midwest Metropole than to cross the median in a Texas prairie or a Mississippi delta town. (America, don't blame it all on your 'Stars and Bars.' Start with your 'Stars and Stripes.')

Ching-In Chen

[as a space to occupy] crossing the source

mash-up harvest from/in response to words
& images of Michael Lin & Nick Cave

in history of skin composition, my mother floats sea
I – I stitch story from your *switchboard* birth mouth
ransack which hair sentence cannot hold your *no operator*

chorus midst a sugar brother
the one in charge of flight

born of paper
a code father made of grains pages keep no mailslot letter bodies

if I – I take your tongue, I ask for his name
he pushes her shoulder past starting line

no exits town

only hair stitch on my tongue
each unchain sentence know no limit
they hold outlets under sea

She could have her own memory To translate :

Floating surface containers
polarized muscle full /thrift museum

in your forage/eye border
300 of a thing provoke
itself as keyhole
but her eye belong

in each ransack morning
I obscure exits
procedure to ransack sentence
each sentence intimate with her chain of command

her hold onto book each stroke
infected with sperm a roof split at river

distance town
letters through mailslot
notice enforce silence
her mouth a river in place

no guests spare chain
separate horizon from infection

What composes town this neck
lace dark owl
a kill cave
burst
flower

two discard
muscle and neck compose
skin

we dance two letters one
story lose ladder

I never really work alone

She whisper full and soft
two rivers into keyhole

a ship make public
highway original live as skin

Two continents stitch each other shut.

Ching-In Chen

hunting ancestors

brittle words
so concerned bottom rivers
ironcast
pot

She walk backwards hard
to open A friend
tells me, I could
your fingers, but there

write poems, I
think. Difficult

in light, graceful

gathering season, everything pick dry. Hungry, my door

step. We
pickle birds
outside
turn a
corner, how you

strain, maybe.
Some days, a line

Ching-In Chen

a lit ghost

winter made me 18 shots a January city ghost
no trees become clear of immigrant

don't tell me who contracts the dawn

no fingerprint speaks to risk the sun with all their
whistle-up boys

don't tell me who shot the drought

with all their flash-
thin voices

don't tell me who clears the coming
with all their pigskin
sold stories

who smooths their cheeks
who turns out to break the news

Ching-In Chen

various various

Not what the captain recorded.

*

My mother bought –
India's west coast, fort wall shoulder
a thousand everyday hands
cutting clay to put on table

*

cities gather to watch divisions *To know absolutely there will be an end to this relationship — apart from keepsakes.*

*

after loud journey and birds

*

die. Suddenly,

imperial decree forced boulevard resurrection

*

Enclaves in english factory ports

*

mouth like a hull
two teeth cracked to sigh

*

Years later, I opened book, wooden box for treasure,
captured lines sank gently to floor.

*

only approachable on foot
network of cities water tanks

*

Stories of this pillar road which ate and ate through ears, toe stubs. I avoided road in my walk to market; a carriage pushed me off home road. Follow tributary into marked section, recently emptied of plague. There were stories.

*

Book begins with epigraph: "every body that is not my body is a foreign country."
Then the water tank a growth I paid for with my eye.

*

Though map muddy, I forced my sore body through pane-glass hedge.
Measured air in my mouth. I missed my eye.

*

Caption — no ear belongs here.

Note
"various various": Italicized words from Daniel Borzutsky's *The Book of Interfering Bodies*, Kimiko Hahn's *The Artist's Daughter*," Shalini Puri's "Canonized Hybridities, Resistant Hybridities: Chutney Soca, Carnival and the Politics of Nationalism"

Bi Sexual

I put my vibrating penis back in the drawer. I know there are men in the world, but I've yet to find one who vibrates. I expect things to be hard. I pay extra for them to vibrate.

Women vibrate hard and I want that about them. They shake and shimmer everything into electricity. Men? Slippery with savior. Mine. And theirs. Who can resist?

Have you heard the one about the girl who really wants a boy but ends up with me? Have you heard the one about the boy who really wants a girl but ends up with me?

A healer once told me I was a threshold for gender. A window boy/girl could slip in and out of to explore the other side. I was both. Never neither.

Out of context I am content. There is an explanation for everything and it's too bad because it's much more interesting when there's not. Take now.

guth rither thor byarner daughter *Gudridur Thorbjarnardottir lived between the cultural worlds of receding Norse paganism and advancing Christianity, and is said to be emblematic of medieval Icelandís restless, brilliant spirit. Sometime before the year 1000, the wealthy and beautiful Thorbjarnardottir married the rich eldest son of Eric the Red. Her imagination was fired by the tales of Eric's second son, Leif Ericson, who had just discovered the New World and come back to Greenland to tell about it. Thorbjarnardottir longed to see the new land, but her husband died before they could get there.*

Fortunately, Thorbjarnardottir, met Thorfinnur, the best sailor of the day. Like her, he had wanderlust. They married and set off across the ocean, found the houses Leif Ericson had built and explored up and down the coast. They settled in what is now Newfoundland, gave birth to a son and stayed about three years. When it was time to leave, they loaded up their Viking ships with goods from the New World, sailed to Norway and sold the exotic materials for a fortune.

Why we wander

This is a story of a woman who loved to live. Who loved to live in this world and so she travelled it. She travelled it so well it took three husbands to keep up with her. Three husbands and a pope. Which depending on how you feel about Catholicism could have more or less weight than three husbands. Which depending on how you feel about heterosexuality, could have more or less weight than the pope.

This is really the story of *the greatest female explorer of all time*. Which is how the president of Iceland described Gudridur Thorbjarnardottir.

The greatest female explorer of all time. I'm sure a lot of other people described her that way too. People that didn't come up right away when I Googled Gudridur.

An even more interesting saga than Leif Erikson someone wrote. Leif Erikson's son was Gudridur's second husband.

I love the name Leif. I always wanted to be named by nature. Leif, River, Sky. Sky Salach. I was let down by my own suburban Schaumburgian Woodfieldmallian name. Cindy.

In the year 2000 a statue was built in Gudridur's honor. A small statue of a tall woman in a Nordic boat with a toddler on her shoulder. Even in the dark stone, her restless, brilliant spirit shines. Even in the dark stone, her son's love for her shines.

The first European woman to give birth on North American soil. The name of Gudridur's first and only son is Snorri. Snorri Thorfinnsson.

This is really the story of a great adventurer who at the end of her husbands became a nun, walked solo to Rome to enlighten the Pope then walked home to live as a hermit in the church that Snorri built for her.

Finding my son has been the adventure of my life. My wanderlust was always for the landscape of the body, the landscape of family. I travelled the straight and narrow for many years, a true adventurer of music and men, until I came upon two roads. I took the sexuality less travelled and that made all the difference.

The terrain of becoming a mother as a lesbian over 40 is not very well mapped. Definitely not for weak. The ambiguous. The catholic.

The short version: After plunging my ex-husband's sperm into myself with a turkey baster in the backseat of my (now ex-) partner's SUV, after shooting myself up with hormones and having my eggs sucked out then placed back in, after pills and fertility charts and acupuncture and stinky tea and doctors shaking their heads, after all that, after everything, Leo.

Leo. Who was not born from my body but of my body. Leo. Who came to us at birth, via his birth mother, who pointed to my picture and said "her."

Who needs a statue after that?

At two years old, he thinks I am a church. His. He doesn't know I travel to my knees each night to thank the world for him. That I pray twice each day for the strength and peace of his body, mind and spirit.

So this is really the story of my son, of whom I am the mother. Because my brain has become something else. It has become his brain. My heart, my lungs, his heart, his lungs. Each regular morning, each sippy of milk, is a tiny new landscape, restless and brilliant. I write poems about it, but really, it's just a day.

Nothing to trek across Rome and tell the pope about. Nothing to drive across town and tell you. And here I am, telling you anyway.

Now go home and call your mothers. Discover something undiscovered about your terrain. Give yourself a nature name.

Worship the world.

cin salach

Now.

When I was 20, my superpower was being 20. I could fly on four hours of sleep a night. Leap tall freshman with nothing to eat but sugarless gumballs. Break through bad grades with an extra semester of easy classes.

When I was 30, my superpower was poetry and music and cigarettes and Sundays at the Green Mill Lounge and boys named Mark and being a blonde. And then a red-head. And then a blonde. And then a red-head.

When I was 40, my superpower was women. Sleeping with them, moving in with them, fighting with them. Then writing poems about sleeping with them, moving in with them and fighting with them.

At 50, my superpower is love. For myself. For everyone really. Even if you piss me off, I'll get over it. I've had that much therapy. It's being young enough to like being old enough. Being more sacred than scared. Drinking more water than wine. And when I wake up, and love is breathing down my neck, I don't toss it off like a blanket.

I pull it on like a cape.

(Cobalt) Thalo Kersey

I Tattooed Jesus

In the tattooing game, sometimes it's all about who you tattooed. Pull rank by the name behind the blood you drew, sometimes it's about talent, sometimes its about proverbial connections, but there's a name game floating about and here's my boast:

I tattooed Jesus.
I found out about this in Past Life Regression Therapy, my therapist Julia delving my subconscious with the precision of a single needle. He came to me Post-Resurrection, showed me the holes ripped into his wrists (I thought, "Suicide?"), told me, in a voice like Texas thunder, to ink "Mary" below each one. A conscientious tattooist, I attempted to dissuade him, told him how people's hearts changed, but

he assured me it was eternal. One Mary for his mom, one for his would-be lover, if his dad hadn't insisted he remain a virgin. I could tell from his face he was too old to be carded, despite still being attached to the apron strings, but since he was both gentle as the lambs that followed him like imprinted ducklings and powerful all the same, I thought he may have some other feminine traits, and ID'd him anyway. As I injected the ink with a gnarled thorn from his crown, he talked to me about his life, his unchaste love for Mary M.,

how sometimes when he turned water into wine he left a little extra water in it, so Peter wouldn't get too plastered, reenacting the scene at the temple where Jesus threw the tables, spilling all the drinks on their robes (with not a Laundromat in sight those days!) It's funny, the magic of tattooing, how secrets sift to the surface. Not like bartenders, who lull diligent defenses into sleep, Daniel's testy lions kept at bay. No, this is confession through pain, the violence of the sacred, the alchemy of skin to a new form of art, the needle transformative, resurrection of

deeply lodged desires into the incarnation of flesh. In this life I tattooed Sheila for hours, watched her grayed eyes burn bright blue as fatigue and pain pinpricked through the usual sarcastic veil over her eyes until the light blazed bright as the Holy Ghost, purified in her own holy blood. She had told me secrets before on lazy smoke breaks in the glass box our job clustered us in, but never one like this, never the truth behind the words, the way she splintered and each

sharp jab of humor poked out from holes carved long ago, punctured by multicolored pills, stolen Everclear, and the sharp, callused knuckles of someone who was supposed to love her. Last week my therapist pressed deeper back, stretching my quiet memories like I stretch skin so the ink will fill the skin fluidly. There we found the Pharaoh Hatshepsut, woman who could not dress as woman and still be in her place of power. She asked me for a discreet cartouche over her hipbone, something no one would see, a hidden revelation known to her flesh but no one else. She wanted the Egyptian equivalent of "Bitch," and when I asked her why, since her reign reigned in peace like a feisty and flighty beast, she answered that those daring enough to risk the rage of the gods whisper under their breath that whether chosen by the deities or not, a woman in control is a bitch. And she supposed she was, by that definition,

a hardcore, in your face, take-this-stereotype-and-shove-it-where-Ra-don't-shine, BITCH. And it was that day, in the therapist's office, listening to the clay and stone fountain gurgling soothingly on the table to my right, that I knew where my fondness for the appellation began. I was proud to be an ink-slinging bitch, territory where few women dare or succeed, I knew myself bold, and beautiful, and in control of ink and flesh and places sometimes even the gods don't walk,

where the profane meets the holy.

Collin Kelley

Girl Detective

Nancy Drew's boyfriend was gay. Her best friends were lesbian lovers. The girl detective chose not to explain these mysteries or redact the evidence. It was the 1930s, after all, when taboos were hip and closets were for clothes. A good investigator always knows how to read between the lines.

Ned Nickerson was the hunky, flaxen-haired do-gooder in a letterman jacket, who lingered too long in the locker room. Back then, tapping heels under bathroom stalls weren't front-page news. Nancy never pressed, accepted his kisses on a turned cheek, her teenage sophisticate coolness a relief. Beards work both ways.

Girly Bess and tomboyish George were inseparable kissing cousins who kept up appearances by dating Emerson College boys, but never let hands wander into their jewel boxes. Feisty fem and judo chopping butch, the perfect, low-maintenance gal pals. Beards work both ways.

And Nancy herself, the confirmed bachelorette with strawberry hair and smart suits, who used her friends as a perfect disguise, to conceal the need for ruin, restraints, secret passages, the desire to be alone in the dark. Maybe diddled by daddy after mommy died, has photos of him schtupping the housekeeper, proof of payoffs and kickbacks – enough dirt to bring River Heights to its knees.

Nancy lords her secrets over them all, but she's no fool. Something lurks in the shadows, immune to her trusty flashlight — the monster that crawled out from under the bed, read her diary, recorded every prayer and sleep-tossed confession. This is a girl acquainted with the night.

Collin Kelley

Revenant

One-upmanship over beer and burgers,
cigarette smoke curling toward scorched ceiling.
We're seat fillers, interchangeable souls going to ash,
tears and queers a dime a dozen here –
can't tell one from the other without a program.

We had sex last night, not with each other,
but we might as well had. It would save us
the trouble of totting up the score,
our extravagant, unquenchable appetites.
I've never been so fat and so empty, I think,
while you casually mention falling off the wagon.
And why not? You're 32 and single again.

It's been a decade since we said goodbye,
when I left you levitating on the floor
in the wake of mushrooms and silver spoons,
and I could take stairs without losing my breath.
When I thought I'd never have sex again
without your face floating above me,
disembodied, superimposed, like smoke
filling my pores and follicles.

Today when I put on my coat,
I caught the scent of last night, of you,
of what cannot ever truly be aired out.
Love does not remain, but every now and then
some random man will touch me
in just the right spot, whisper his desires,
and you will surface, a revenant
impervious to exorcism,
even when I call some other's name.

Eduardo C. Corral

Ceremonial

Delirious,
touch-starved,
I pinch a mole

on my skin, pull it
off, like a bead —

I pinch & pull until
I am holding
a black rosary. Prayer
will not cool

my fever.
Prayer will not

melt my belly fat,
will not thin
my thighs.

A copper-
faced man once
called me beautiful.
Stupid,
stupid man.

I am obese. I am
worthless.
I can still feel
his thumb —
warm,
burled — moving

in my mouth.
His thumbnail
a flake

of sugar
he would not
allow me to swallow.
Desperate
for the sting of snow
on my skin,
rosary
tight in my fist,
I walk into

a closet, crawl
into a wedding dress.
Oh Lord,
here I am.

Eduardo C. Corral

Guillotine

The scorpions always arrive
at dawn. Gently,
with their pincers,
they touch the cuts
on my lips. I clutch

the edges
of the mattress, stare

at the mirrored ceiling.
My mouth opens,
but no sound staggers out.
The scorpions —

dark green, dank —
reach in, pull out

the razor blade
under my tongue...
Two scorpions.

A razor blade.
Slowly, in unison,
without letting go of the metal,
they move.
A little guillotine
making its way

down my body.
I remember
dragging my thumb
through his beard,

coppery & difficult.
The scorpions pause
on my chest,
tilt the razor blade.
A threat, a reminder.
It's my task to stop yearning
for as long
as it takes them

to carry a razor blade
across my skin.
My thoughts surge & swerve
from monsoon storms

to accordions
to pecan groves.

The little guillotine
starts moving again.
I begin to sense

the enormity of my body.
The razor blade
high in the air.
For now.

Eduardo C. Corral

Sentence

I crawl back   he unpacks his tools
oils the wooden handles   rinses the metal

fragrant   his thighs fragrant his sneer

koi & infinity inked on his skin   an ecstatic
blue a bewildered green

some wounds are ovals some wounds are opals
the ears of a white wolf pivot   toward the moon

I flee now & then   alone in the desert for months
a nomad in a kimono of pressed-together dust

beautiful his throat his words   even more beautiful
"it's my turn to ask for a bit more from you"

he likes it when I bleed   strangers once

gently he hammers gold into a sentence   gently
the sentence enters me

after Don McKay

Elizabeth Bradfield

Dispatch from This Summer

— Lymantria dispar dispar

Frayed, moth-eaten, vulnerable. Those Florida dancers
gunned down & my young self coming out dancing & pathetic
fallacy (*dispar dispar*) crawls all over June's fresh oaks,

gnawing them to a February canopy. The news, bad
oracle, gnaws fact & rumor. Above, unrelenting
mastication, defoliation. *Lymantria,* 'destroyer,' all else gone,

you hump up even the stiff needles of pines. What will happen
come winter, no sun stored? Should we spray? Should
we shun social media? Avoid large aggregations? How

hot the birds must be, unshaded in their nests. (Guilty
thrill of peering down on them, black-billed cuckoos calling.)
Other wings. The white towering stagecraft of angels

sentry at Orlando's mourning. We consider what it would take
to pick the trees clean. Could we? The bark the grass the ground
writhes. In a grove in China, a grim documentary:

honeybees gone, people pollinate fruit trees by hand. I twitch away
from one caterpillar dangling from its thread, hanging by
the silk that brought it here, to the New World, to Massachusetts

even, because some merchant in 1869—while Grant
took the presidency and Elizabeth Cady Stanton spoke
before Congress and the Golden Spike was hammered

into Utah and the South fumbled through what's called
Reconstruction—thought *crop, harvest, riches* & hoped
the long, expensive trek to mulberry unnecessary. We gnaw

through news feeds. We post & share, unsure
if we are offering or consuming. In the forest, a constant
heavy frass. On my side of the river, healthy trees. Oak leaves

thick and dark. In the dance clubs near me, there is
dancing. But introduction, dispersal. In the week
after Pulse, in Massachusetts, 450% more guns like that gun

were sold. If you can stand to walk a narrow path through the leafless
forest, you can arrive at a circle of water that will allow your body
to be beautifully held, whoever you are. It's true, you'll have to return

by the same path, go back through those apocalyptic trees. If
I had waited a month to begin this poem, I would have begun
with the re-leafing, fuzzed red growth in late July, moth-flutter

among the trunks not angelic but like paper corners that didn't
get burned in someone's attempted or accidental. Is it too late?
Now, plastered to bark, the russet humps of eggs that I scrape with a stick
— vengeful, hopeful, despairing — even as they are being laid.

— North Truro, 2016

Elizabeth Bradfield

Learning to Swim

— after Bob Hicok & Aricelis Girmay

Now forty-five, having outlasted some of
myself, I must reflect: what if I hadn't been held
by my mom in the YWCA basement
pool, her white hands slick under

my almost-toddler armpits, her thumbs
and fingers firm around my ribs, which
is to say my lungs, held gently as a liverwurst
sandwich and pulled, kindly, under?

What if I hadn't been taught to trust
water might safely erase me those years
I longed to erase or at least abandon care of
my disoriented, disdained body? I might have

drowned instead of just ebbed, never slid
from given embankments into this other
natural course.
                    Drift and abundance
in what she shared. The wider ocean
of trade and dark passage not yet

mine to reckon. And so even now, sharp salt
of other waters known to my mouth, I am
afloat, skin-chilled, core-warm, aware
of what lurks, glad I was shown

how to hold and help another
in our improbable buoyancy.

Elizabeth Bradfield

Regarding the Absent Heat of Your Skin on Letters I Receive While at Sea

Paper wing   Words smudged
in your hand's stroke   What
has been sealed   Torn mouth

Lung-must

And a shiver along
my lateral line, olfactory
lobe lit up

Breath on the paper
Wind on the water (& off it)
Breath from the water
And ill wind   Tear-salt

Fish near the surface, glinting
Plankton rising   forced

Scent of panic   (lung-must)
Petrels arrive because of
Patter and feed

Your eyes on the horizon
are greedy, could eat
leagues   Call my name

Breeze   Wind   Gale
Let the air clock around your mouth

It pushes, unturned,
against your mouth

If you stand on the shore and call
I'll know

Elizabeth Bradfield

Neko Harbor

Here. The anticipated harbor. Here where Lynne Cox swam 1.22 miles. Pushed heart pushed breath pushed self against cold's hard shove. A deep thrum to enter water she entered. Peer out cargo door, suss which gloves, boots, hat the day needs. Water dimensional with brash, growlers, bergs. H saw the biggest calving of her life here — nearly the glacier's whole face. Surge wrapped the point. Everyone speed-stumbled into boats (none lost). To have seen it. Interminable thundered slump, hump of water mounding out high, higher, ephemeral drumlin of sea and ice. Other stories heave to mind, trees wave-snapped at 1,720 feet in Lituya. Flare a stern-facing deckhand spotted as we rode the brash-swell out of Tracy Arm (turn, rescue, shore-hauled boat wrecked). This harbor bowl musters it all: history, ice, us, crabeaters, terns, my yearning.

prop bangs ice all afternoon

— strange morse — no one seems to care

so I keep going

Note: The long-distance swimmer Lynne Cox has swum amazing distances across many of the world's oceans. Although her swim in Neko Harbor was not long, it was long to be immersed in water of that temperature without a wet suit. On July 9, 1958, after an earthquake caused a rockslide, the largest wave in modern history occurred in Lituya Bay, on the northern Southeast Alaska coast about halfway between Cape Spencer and Yakutat.

Ellen Bass

Taking Off the Front of the House

I'm at the kitchen table, drinking strong tea, eating eggs
with poppy-gold yolks from our chickens, Marilyn and Estelle.
There's a red car parked across the street and my neighbor's gorgeous irises,
their frilled tongues tasting the air.
"Monsanto is suing Vermont," I say, turning the pages of *The Times.*
I say it loud because Janet's in the living room
in the faded chair the cat has scratched into hay
eating yogurt and the strawberries she brought home from the field
where she labors to relieve the tender berry of its heavy chemical load.
"What?" she says. She isn't wearing her hearing aids
so I take a breath and project my voice. And as I enunciate the corporate evils,
suddenly the front of the house is sheared away.
We're on a stage, the audience seated on the asphalt of Younglove Avenue,
watching this quirky couple eat their breakfast and yell
back and forth from one room to another.
And throughout the day, as I throw a load of laundry
in the drier, answer the phone, as Janet lies on the couch
reading *Great Expectations* and we bicker
about the knocking in the pipes and whether we really need to call a plumber,
I admire how the actor who plays the character of me
and the actor who plays the character of her
perform our parts so perfectly
in this production that will last
just a little while before it closes for good.
And when night comes, we smoke a little weed — something called
Thunder Fuck,
which must be someone's high opinion of himself,
but in truth is quite nice, though we only take a couple tokes
since Janet's on blood pressure medication and she can't
do the way she did at twenty when she slung a goatskin bag
over her shoulder and wandered around Senegal in flip-flops.
As I reach for her, she says, "Now the audience can sit on the back deck

by the barbeque and this play can be called
The Old Lesbians Go to Bed at the End of the Day.
I light the candle her mother gave me for my last birthday when she could
still put on her lipstick and Janet pushed her around the store in her
wheelchair.
And the dog's still on his mat on the floor of the closet because he's afraid
of firecrackers and took up sleeping there last 4th of July on top of the shoes.
The set is authentic—a messy stack of books on my nightstand,
on her side, reading glasses and the hearing aids that sit there all day.
And as she turns toward me and I feel again
the marvelous architecture of her hips, the moon,
that expert in lighting, rises over the roofline,
flooding us in her old, flawless silvery wash.

Ellen Bass

God and the G-Spot

"He didn't want to believe. He wanted to know."
— Ann Druyan, Carl Sagan's wife, on why he didn't believe in God

I want to know too. Belief and disbelief
are a pair of tourists standing on swollen feet
in the Prado — *I don't like it.*
I do. — before the Picasso.

Or the tattoo artist with a silver stud
in her full red executive lips,
who, as she inked in the indigo blue, said,
I think the G-spot's one of those myths
men use to make us feel inferior.

God, the G-spot, falling in love. The earth round
and spinning, the galaxies speeding
in the glib flow of the Hubble expansion.
I'm an East Coast Jew. We all have our opinions.

But it was in the cabin at La Selva Beach
where I gave her the thirty tiny red glass hearts
I'd taken back from my husband when I left.
He'd never believed in them. She, though, scooped
them up like water, let them drip through her fingers
like someone who has so much she can afford to waste.

That's the day she reached inside me
for something I didn't think I had.
And like pulling a fat shining trout from the river
she pulled the river out of me. That's
the way I want to know God.

Ellen Bass

The Small Country

Unique, I think, is the Scottish *tartle,* that hesitation
when introducing someone whose name you've forgotten

And what could capture *cafuné*, the Brazilian Portuguese way to say
running your fingers, tenderly, through someone's hair?

Is there a term in any tongue for choosing to be happy?

And where is speech for the block of ice we pack in the sawdust of our hearts?

What appellation approaches the smell of apricots thickening the air
when you boil jam in early summer?

What words reach the way I touched you last night—
as though I had never known a woman—an explorer,
wholly curious to discover each particular
fold and hollow, without guide,
not even the mirror of my own body.

Last night you told me you liked my eyebrows.
You said you never really noticed them before.
What is the word that fuses this freshness
with the pity of having missed it.

And how even touch itself cannot mean the same to both of us,
even in this small country of our bed,
even in this language with only two native speakers.

Ellen Bass

Ode to Repetition

I like to take the same walk
down the wide expanse of Woodrow to the ocean,
and most days I turn left toward the lighthouse.
The sea is always different. Some days dreamy,
waves hardly waves, just a broad undulation
in no hurry to arrive. Other days the surf's drunk,
crashing into the cliffs like a car wreck.
And when I get home I like
the same dishes stacked in the same cupboards
and then unstacked and then stacked again.
And the rhododendron, spring after spring,
blossoming its pink ceremony.
I could dwell in the kingdom of Coltrane,
those rivers of breath through his horn,
as he forms each phrase of "Lush Life"
over and over until I die. Once I was afraid
of this, opening the curtains every morning,
only to close them again each night.
You could despair in the fixed town of your own life.
But when I wake up to pee, I'm grateful
the toilet's in its usual place, the sink with its gift of water.
I look out at the street, the halos of lampposts
in the fog or the moon rinsing the parked cars.
When I get back in bed I find
the woman who's been sleeping there
each night for thirty years. Only she's not
the same, her body more naked
in its aging, its disorder. Though I still
come to her like a beggar. One morning
one of us will rise bewildered
without the other and open the curtains.
There will be the same shaggy redwood
in the neighbor's yard and the faultless stars
going out one by one into the day.

Farah Milagros Yamini

Thirteen Ways of Looking at an Ass

I.
A woman and her ass
are not one.
A woman, her ass,
and an onlooker
are one.

II.
The derrière raises fists,
punching through loose linens.
It resists attempts to obscure it.

III.
O, European butts and designers,
why do you keep us out
of your Zara pant club?

Do you not see how
big bottom petals
amplify the Hibiscus'
filaments?

The ones
dispersing
golden
dust.

IV.
When we talk
to most straight males
the most memorable point
of the conversation

is behind us.

V.
We'd prefer if there were no assholes
in this poem.

VI.
A big butt means floating
at the beach. It means
our limbs are an open yawn
above the ocean floor.

VII.
On the toilet.
Blood vessels rupture.
Could someone show
cis straight men
how it feels like
to let someone
penetrate you
and be
penetrated?

IX.
At the feel of fingerlings
trailing the sunrise of this backside,
we are the most beloved womyn
crying out
softly, softly.

X
We do not know which to prefer,
the feel of backside biceps in goddess pose
or the swing of the fleshy tambourine
in half moon.

XI.
She floated in
strong spine and soft eyes
marking the edge
of earth.

Rumpus first
I moonwalk.

XII
I know noble accents
and innuendoes
but the workers
didn't use any. In bullhorn voices
they announce our *culo.*

We don't react
to demonstrate our cool-oh-ness.

XIII.
We were of one mind.
Walking like a triangle
head held high by two buns.

Farah Milagros Yamini

Speaking Between My Soul and Sexy Parts

For Miami's many tongues & my grandmother,
the polyglot Alexandrian

Shakespeare trató de hablar del amor only in English:
Love is a smoke and is made with the fume of sighs
but how much sexier is the three-tongues-in-one-phrase:
L'amore e un fumo hecho del vapor de sighs?

What can I say? After being raised by my loving, polyglot grandmother
who answered my questions like this:
"ta bon" followed by
idiomatically
incorrect English, and ended with a "¿vale?"
my soul and sexy parts now crave more
from language.

So when my smartpretty lover, Chérie,
is away vacationing in Latin America while
I vacation in Miami's premier hospital, Mt.Sinai,
I am eager to counteract the icy
hospital air with language-roses and romance.

I find Chérie on FB messenger and begin to write:
"I love that you are full of sorpesas para la mulher"

They say,
"Cada uno tiene su estilo
pero mi cachondear
es preguntar y preguntar."

I say
"When Plath writes
that every woman adores a fascist
the boot in the face
the brute"
The missing
sincere-half is
"every woman adores a feminist/the question marks only she/gets to answer."

Still, I want more than this.
I love language and tongues
so much
that I insist
"if you want to excite my sexy parts
stuff several lenguas en une phrase."

Chérie says
"being asked for cosas sucias is pretty sweet."

And, suddenly, it doesn't matter that I'm in a hospital,
or that there's a hundred and one messes that need attention.
Suddenly, all that matters is that there is a feminist
waiting for my answers,
y eso es muy gostoso.
A sound for my sore, polyglot ears.

Gem Blackthorn

Dissociative Sexuality Disorder

Vox populi will point to the DSM-lies and say I
am a manufactured psychiatric phenomenon.
I'm a maligned heterosexual.
I'm a maligned homosexual.
That I splinter into multiple identities,
like tree branches, whenever
I take up a new lover.

Alter One likes the CrossFit alpha male kings,
Alter Two likes the ballerinas bobbing around
bookstore bookshelves, dancing.
And they can't fathom integration.
That one mind has the capacity to love across genders.

My voice dries like the ink on the institutional paperwork
prescribing a treatment of hypnosis torture
in search of a trauma that never was.
They commit me to their therapy
until I become one, and
blackout the other.

And so, for my sanity, I lie.
I become two.

Gerry Gomez Pearlberg

OCTO9

... hay barcos que buscan ser mirados para poder hundirse tranquilos.
... there are ships that want to be seen in order to sink in peace.
— Lorca, *from* "Moon and Panorama of Insects"

Grey, static sea I hold before me like a microphone. But indolence
doesn't listen, it's too busy lapping the edges, trying to extract
the bare minimum from any situation. So here I sit, covered
in sand, crying over a lost androgyny, my apathy
to gender which once held so much promise.
Hobby, trinket, snow-choked hamlet.
In this place, a job (like gender)
is something to "hold down."
It's usually the other way
around, the phrase
almost human
truly an in-
sult.
Listen up:
here's to some luck
in attaining a clue. Start
where you are, kissing the
whimper of every startled animal,
webbed foot, hoof, fin. The new crew-
cut of which you're so proud, experienced
knuckles, well-filed lesbian fingernails... they've
taken you just about everywhere & it's smooth sailing
from here: Animaline. "Dynamic lethargy" is how Burton
described Eastwood, a spider's indolence, a shiftless montage.
If "Yanks have tails" & "Jews got horns," what's potent enough to
rinse the grit from your brain-stem? *It wasn't that you were a bad kid,*
Mom said, *just that it was hard to follow where you were going.*
Where was I? The time was 1970, 15 years after the invention
of "Cool" & I was nine. Panavision Reflex was in its heyday

filming our society after the bomb, pure macho. Is that
why I longed for horns & was so hard to swallow?
I wished each dawn for antlers to rise upon my
head, a velvet chandelier: stubborn, baroque,
a manifestation of mind—signal of my
improvident aberrance—willing &
able to stake out a territory I
could call mine. I never
felt fully part of this
world. That's not
a bad thing. I
followed
where I was
going, longed like
a lizard to drop my tail—
go hybrid—a composite creature
in a children's book, a horizontal slash
across my pages, where head & torso might
become a goat or frog or terror, & down below
a kicking bear. I wanted to be the jellyfish (Hydro-
medusa; Man-of-War) whose tentacled skirt lashed out
& stung the numbing scenery while back upstairs the wild
bull gored open its world of platters & false answers: my plaza.
Because gender, though illustrious, just wasn't giving up her clues.
In that context I wanted not the golden keys to the kingdom but a Talking
GI Joe—the 14 holes in his chest a spatter of gore-wounds, neat &
perfect—opposite of any war—a sieve through which the 7
seas of language roared their static monologues. I wanted
better, but he was a sailor on the open sore of sea.
I aimed to be lost in a bigger story than that
which girlhood normally receives, adding

my own embellishments, trading in de-
pendency for a more legitimate
principle: Surprise! To love
the tale & live to tell it.
But there was
biology
to contend with
& science can squelch
you harder, faster, more
obliquely than even gender. We
give it such power. I turned away
from it—one less wrong road to go down
—& traced instead a loner's sense of justice.
I walked the pebbly beach, rarely found it serene
or streamlined. It was active, implicating everything.
Physical power & the capacity to act from that place has
sickened me since I was young & fell for tadpoles. I mean for
a collaboration with stillness that lasts a lifetime. No more, no less,
no brain-dead gawking. That means a willingness to be accused of under-
acting. Let me take a moment to acknowledge my debts. I'll do it
silently, like a director: "Very little fill into the shadows to let
the shadows speak." For surely you realize that where we're
headed is best if turned away from. The limits of a hero
are the clues to my character. Beginning without you,
tomorrow begins, snarling or wagging or drooling
at the sky. Clouds like antlers lodged in high
branches, picked almost clean—just a trace
of meat left on the skull, a little
meat & fur, an eyebrow
raised in genuine
disbelief at
destiny.

Animals are
so earnest. What can't
we learn from them? Even
their skulls convey great delicacy
of mind, attentiveness. I'm fully fledged
now, a frog pushing dinner down with either
eyelid: I squint at what I've swallowed & put aside,
a self-created image with patience enough to let stillness
come through everything else: a unifying theory for absolutely
everything in the universe. I am a kind of Eastwood, facing all directions
as global extinctions fly in the face of my world in many grand &
tiny guises. I aim at the onslaught in a last heartfelt gesture—
no clowning around—the dusk on my boots I sleep in.
When the badge is tossed, it's up to you to read
between the lines. The cup of atonement
is a moon-flower in mud, indigo-open,
ready to take on the trees with stoic
tendrils, pushing skyward, a
harrowing arrow.
Withdrawn
from the buckskin
quiver, who really cares
how badly you're portrayed?
Reckless. Arrogant. Cranky. Chaste.
Choose your weapon. You talk a lot about
days without rules but look how you're living.
Without pity for yourself, or mercy for anyone in
the line of fire. Or maybe it's a lie, a shadow you filled
in simply for effect or the sheer pleasure of erasing it later:
a woman's power. No one who has truly lived remains indigenous.
Nothing—not even the sea—is static. If you listen hard, the shadows give

their opinions. I look them in the eye & like the shadows speak,
filling myself in as surely as the ocean swallows every hole
of silent sand, storing it behind the eyes through which
the 7 seas do follow. No mark is truly permanent.
To thyself be indigenous. Be indigenous to
the world. I lay down my swagger,
sword to plough-share at
ocean's edge, where
gender smirks
back into me
before the
last
autopsy, for
there have been
many. My swagger
undulates—bruised seahorse
in the ripples—crying out so tenderly
as it drowns, I'm almost tempted to save it.
No. I lower the dagger on which I impaled my life
in waiting, O elusive, golden lyre. I pull myself through
the repossessed music & aim my last arrow toward translucence of purpose.

Gregg Shapiro

How To Flirt

Listen to Doris Day singing, "Once
I had a secret love," no more
than 214 times a day or an amount
equal to your heartbeat on an especially
loathsome or love-soaked Valentine's
Day when you were nine or nineteen years
old. Avoid singing or humming "Que Sera
Sera" like a cheating ex. Otherwise "whatever
will be" won't be. Bat your eyes but try not to
think about baseball bats, Christian Bale

as Batman, vampire bats or batty old ladies
like Aunt Clara on "Bewitched." Be bewitching
without twitching or casting an irreversible
spell. Spell it out in letters big enough
to read from a great distance. Keep
your distance from boxes of chocolates, bouquets
of flowers, anything associated with allergies
and fevers of the flesh. Flesh out as much
as you can about his past, your past
lives lived among roaming tribes, romantic

royalty, plundering pirates or tricky tricks.
Obsess over his handsome profile
on social media sites you wouldn't
ordinarily frequent without an experienced
guide, instruction manual or some form
of protection. Frequently check your breath,
your pulse, your email and phone, your hair
in anything reflective, with the exception
of his mirrored sunglasses. Dress for sex, for
success, to impress. Don't forget to wear

clean underwear. Remember what your mother
told you about reckless drivers and crosswalks.
Cross with the light, cross your heart and hope
to die of embarrassment if he ever sees you
crossing your heart. Hide the doodles, the scrawled
hearts on binders and spiral notebook covers
containing the swirly equation of your initials
in a place so secure that even you have trouble
remembering where it is. Cover your ass. Remember,
he doesn't even know you're alive.

Gregg Shapiro

Dedicated Driver

(after Denise Duhamel)

At the Aventura Mall, wandering the luminous and cacophonous corridors, window shopping at Louis Vuitton, the Apple Store and Y3 by Yohji Yamamoto, eyeing the delicacies at the food court (a $10 milk shake at Häagen-Dasz!), clutching a personally inscribed copy of Denise's new book of poems, catching up on past and present health crises, watching a zombie rom-com, you don't think anything could possibly dampen your mood. Not even the momentary panic of not being able to find your cars in the labyrinthine parking structures. But you've been wrong before. The text letting you know that you're expected to make an appearance at Tropics, where those waiting for you have already been situated for a couple of gin-soaked hours, causes you to miss your exit at Sunrise. You're getting better at navigating 95 and the Oakland Park off-ramp comes up quickly. A metered parking space in front of the bar is taken as a good sign, although that could go either way, too. Once inside, you take stock of the looming potential disasters. Your husband ensconced at the piano bar, singing show-tunes. Your sister-in-law and niece, faces flushed, all garbled speech and wild hair, are the picture of plastered delight. Novices to gay bar culture, they've made fast friends with the equally pickled patrons and overly accommodating wait-staff. But your sister-in-law has had enough of the showy belters and wants to go country line-dancing. Weaving unsteadily out onto the sidewalk, where their carriage and driver awaits, it's less than five minutes to the next whiskey bar. At the aptly named

Scandals, with your trio of passengers, who have ordered another trio of drinks, you run into some people you know visiting from Chicago. After introductions are made, first you are credited with being the desiccated driver, then the dedicated driver. When you correct the slurred slurs, getting your proper due as the designated driver, you soberly think to yourself, this is why I don't drink, why I never drank. But this is before the twirled and twisted two-step becomes a two-person pile-up on the dance floor. Before the broken glass and spilled cocktail, the raised voices and disoriented disagreement at the poker table. Before you quietly slip out after making sure they have cab fare, before the phone rings and they ask you if you've taken off your hat for the night. Before you pick them up, just north of the 6th Avenue bridge and return them safely and soundly home.

Gregg Shapiro

My Mother's Vanity

There was a mascara smear on one of the monogrammed pink hand towels. It was in the shape of a child's primitive rendering of a tree; leafless in autumn. You might think, "That's a lot of mascara," and it was.

What made it worse was that I denied having anything to do with it. Novice liar. Who else could have done it? Did I think my mother was that oblivious? She always made sure to wipe the peach lipstick streaks from the mouthpiece after she hung up the white princess phone. I was the one who regularly forgot to do the same.

I'll say this. I knew enough to stay out of her closet, away from her clothes. The bras and panties and girdles and garters, the stockings and tights, the negligees and nightgowns from Schwartz's Intimate Apparel held no interest. Neither did coulottes, see-through and opaque blouses in silk, rayon and cotton, colorful pantsuits and jumpsuits, clam diggers, mini, midi or maxi skirts, dresses, plaid or striped slacks, jumpers, cashmere and angora sweaters, pastel shells or patterned shifts, corduroy and denim blazers.

Sure, I might slip a bare foot into a stiletto heel, a pump or strappy sandal. She had small feet; we were practically the same size. I avoided the zip-up wet-look boots in white, black, fire-engine red and sky blue. I worried about stuck zippers. I didn't want to get into something I couldn't get out of quickly.

But how could I avoid her vanity? The tortoise shell comb, the matching onyx hairbrush and hand mirror, the hair clips and pins, the clip-on bows and velvet headbands. My thick, pitch black hair a shimmering reflection of her regularly dyed coif; dark and resilient as black lacquer.

Was it my artistic streak that led me to swirl fingers, brushes and other applicators in the powdery terrains of rouge, blush and eye shadow? Imagine the eyelid as a canvas. A blank slate beckoning for color and contrast. Eyebrow pencils in their own murky hues. Cool and damp eyeliner, outlining and emphasizing.

Lipstick tubes containing vaguely phallic rockets of tint and shade, iridescent and ethereal or bright and flushed. The waxy warmth caressing and coloring lips, accentuating kisses, puckers, smiles and frowns. Every lip-printed tissue was stashed and trashed.

No wonder they call the device used to apply mascara a wand. It contains magical powers, transforming lashes that are too short, too light, too limp, too wispy into sculpture. Even the shyest eyes command attention when lashes are darkened and dramatically drawn out, like living picture frames. The sensation of dipping the bristles into the tube and gently dragging the brush along the fine hairs is electrically charged.

Next came the masking of the faintly chemical smell of the palette's potions. So many pretty bottles in such distinctive shapes; Tigress and Woodhue by Faberge, Jean Nate, Estee Lauder, Topaz by Avon, Halston, and Jovan's Musk Oil. Pulse points. So little goes such a long way.

Her jewelry box had a similar effect. How else to complete the process? Bangles and beads, costume jewelry and clip-on earrings. Gemstones and rhinestones. Pearls and plastic geometric shapes. Cocktail rings and chokers. Gold and silver-plated baubles. Multi-colored bubble watches for wrists. Chains and strands, and timepieces worn as necklaces.

Did I feel cute? Desirable? Seductive? Glamorous? New each time? Indestructible? Older than my single digit age? You bet I did.

That time that the handsome bearded guy at the indoor flea market told me I was pretty enough to be a girl, my father went ashen. I didn't even have a lick of make-up on my face. Maybe I didn't need it after all. Maybe I just needed to stand still and be adored for my natural beauty, something on which neither my mother nor father could agree. I was the perfect blend of their facial features, skin tones, hair texture; all in miniature. They always looked at me as if they couldn't decide if that worked in my favor or theirs.

One day I got careless, sloppy, reckless. One day was all it took. For someone so good at making sure that compacts clicked shut silently, that glass bottles never clinked, that lipstick points never dulled, that eyebrow pencils stayed sharpened and the shavings were properly disposed of, that no speck of powder, no matter how pale, was left behind, I really blew it.

Cold cream was involved. Soap and water, too. Foam and scrubbing. Something stinging in my eye. More warm water. The burning sensation subsided although the blurred vision persisted. Reaching for something terry-cloth soft to dry and comfort. Something left behind.

I was watching television or reading a book. I was drawing a picture of a face, not mine, or coloring in one in a coloring book. I was making paper snowflakes or construction paper links. I was building something with Lego blocks or Lincoln Logs or playing with Matchbox or Hot Wheels cars when my mother called me into the bathroom and pointed to the monogrammed hand towel, now monogrammed with something else.

I lied. I denied. I whined. I cried. I ranted. I recanted. I stomped my feet. I folded my arms. Tears fell. Snot bubbled and dripped from my nose. It tasted like perjury.

What else could I do on that day but destroy the evidence? Piles of Maybelline, Cover Girl, Max Factor, Revlon, Helena Rubinstein and Yardley products heaped in the center of my parents' king size bed. Every bottle of perfume poured out as an accelerant. The offending towel ignited by my father's butane lighter and dropped where it could do the most damage. I would use the ashes like kohl to enhance my eyes, my best feature, blinking and glowing as the house blazed and melted around me.

Holly Iglesias

Reliquary

It was still life after she'd gone — hair in the brush, scented talc, the impress of her younger self in the cushions of the couch. Her departure called for elegy, which swelled with great speed into epic until it burst, and, exhausted, fell, settling like a tissue-wrapped ringlet slipt free from the pages of *Sonnets from the Portuguese.*

Holly Iglesias

Word Bank

1. *Migration* arrives in the 17th century, in reference first to people, then animals.

2. The *vagrant* lacks a fixed abode and thus wanders.

3. Coined under Louis XIV, *refugee* describes one seeking asylum —

4. We call the mid-19th century wave of revolutions *Springtime of the Peoples.*

5. But what of the Hunger and *blight* expanding from a plant disease to that which withers hope?

— then shifts during the Great War to one fleeing *home.*

Holly Iglesias

The Game of Crones

Dungeons & Dragons pulled our children through the haze of the Reagan years. It gave them something to do as we watched TV in a jug-wine stupor — evangelists warning of end days, another tiny dictator in the Dade County jail, the dawn of aerobics. They developed plots deep into the night; their homework suffered. All we could do was peek through the blinds as helicopter searchlights strafed the neighborhood.

Tonight at the Crow & Quill Public House, post-apocalyptic youth concoct attars of the past — Weimar waifs, Dharma bums, Kewpie dolls, the last Doobie Brother — expressing in costume virtue spoiled and vice redeemed. All they need now is the lusty monk.

Holly Iglesias

Angelus Novus

The Angel of History must look just so.
—Walter Benjamin

To ease the pain, he evokes the Klee caged in his mind, converting the image to text, scratching left to right, left to right. The room reeks of romance, but this lust for the past, for the erotics of time and its beautiful damage, is what wounds him. He stares at her face and she stares back, a rose window bereft of glass, wings singed by future winds, the heap of spires and thrones, satchels and bones, mounting at her feet.

James Allen Hall

The Saw

Galeria Hermandad, Toledo

A hand hammered flat this hot length of iron,
cut one side a jagged row of teeth.

The criminal was tied by his feet, inverted,
the saw at his scrotum. The act required two men,

before and aft, straining through flesh,
their breath ragged. All because

he'd followed through cobblestone streets
a plainclothes soldier home. Kissed him

open-eyed. Saw night shredded down
to morning. Saw too late in his lover's closet

the row of uniforms, legs halved by hanging,
same uniforms come to break in the door,

carrying his kicking legs to the public square where
they washed the saw before they started cutting. *Sierra.*

My lover corrects my r's. We're standing
in dry museum light, in Toledo,

hands pressed on the stained glass windows
of the wrong century. Behind glass, a row of white

pontiff hoods, preserved, eyeing my wrists.
Last night I was suspect, he played guard,

tying me down, my body made to receive, his
to inflict. It took hours to re-enter myself.

Now, in the museum, I want to be wrong
about the man, about the ecstasy

in pain, the feeling there's something
in this world that loves me, cut apart.

James Allen Hall

Stock Character

Jumped from the bridge, the top of the building,
jumped in front of a train, a bus, out the window

into a noose hanging from the barn rafter, noose
in the dim closet, noose made of bed sheets, threadbare

hotel towels, hanging from the doorjamb, the tree
house out back, hanging from an oak in the thicket

we see only from a distance, only after the shot
reports, birds scattering up into gray air, metaphor

for the body collapsing to the ground
where he will not be buried, but burned.

James Allen Hall

Irregular Plurals

A pile of sticks bound for the pyre—
it's easy to forget *faggot* is already plural.

Every plural scissors its singular,

everything pieces back to one,
the problem of oranges and orchard,
the problem a cut apple spits out to its seeds.

Example: the plural of story is history.

I is ad infinitum. The plural of thinking
is feeling. My problem is the article I
read yesterday about the window and the boy.
I'll come back for them. I'm sorry

I can't stop a thing from accumulating.

Add an –s, an –es. Archaic, how we think
adding more makes a story bearable.
The plural of broken is suicide. The plural
of string is harping, just as the plural
of hand is jobs. Shiver of. Quiver in.

There is no one pleasure when words fail.

This is true of pain as well, and that is
the plural of epiphany. It feels monstrous
to be saved more than once, so the plural
of we must be Jesus. The plural of once
I was raped is every day after.
The plural victim growing inside me, garden

proliferating past its seed. Think

of the sixteen-year-old boy, jumping
from the building's fourth-story window,
limbs seeking singularity the moment
the john unties the restraints that keep him
the plural of bed. Cruelty is its own plural.
It makes me glad to say he survived,
that boy is somewhere breathing, making

my lives shudder into focus, all too clear.

James Allen Hall

An American Porn Star Contemplates the Divine

Call your God of mourning, of longing, but I claim a God
who wants us returned to the mind instead of the world
that locks us in, the God who made every cage
with a keyhole, taking the body as blueprint.

Sometimes I wonder what kind of anal sex God has.

Sometimes my mother sits smoking on her end of the phone
saying, *Aren't you ashamed of yourself?* Then, *I've never
had an orgasm*, crying on my bed after my father's funeral.
He wanted to be cremated, she buried him in a dirt hole.
I am ashamed I didn't make the world filthier
so people could enjoy it more. Shame God made last.

Tuesday, another jock-themed shoot,
lights rebounding off rented lockers, I can't stay hard.
Maybe I've finally pissed God off, he's taken away
my one redeeming talent. The boom guy withdraws
his flaccid mic, the director thunders off to find some Cialis.

I look good in surrender.

Later, in an airport Starbucks, JFK-bound, a man in line
pays for me. *I've seen all your movies,* tonguing his bottom lip
like I'm a thin film of cherry-flavored gloss.
Something in me that is afraid to be naked and is naked
wants to ask him, this needlessly bowtied traveler,
How was I?—Just to remember myself

someone's deity. In the movie they make
with my body, I say *Oh God* like it's a threat.
Should I feel punished no one comes home with me

after the discoball goes out? I baptize one cigarette
with the end of another, stumble into a taxi,
its leather-backed seat slit, soft foam spilling out.

Sometimes my scene boyfriend smiles goofy up at me,
his tongue lolling at the corner, and I forget the camera
catching us is the eye of God. He made us like a virus:

what's human is incurable, undetectable, subject to time.

James Allen Hall

Stock Character

There is a pyre of unsayable things inside me,
stacked, darkened with gasoline. I varnish
the wood to mask's shine — now I'm *fairy decorator*,
now *tortured musician*. I demand my piano.

I play a song that a fop, a fool can loosen his ascot,
can jitter to. I do like a tea dance. I do like a pair
of booty shorts and how the body swings them alive.
I am mask wearing mask. All I can show is

— *ta da* — I'm all show queen. I like a plot twist
arch as any eyebrow, yet I end every story hanged,
knifed, run over in traffic, blood-spattered
spectacle. It isn't the character

(femme muscle bear), the locale (your place,
silly), or the costume (see shorts, above, left
behind), but the story that traps me. I'm so good
at Man with Gun at His Temple, Man With Pills,

Man Terminal with American Imagination
Debilitates me Syndrome. It's like I
invented him, the only lovelorn prophet
in a romantic comedy so stale it needs death

to liven things up. But I can't just waltz in
and tell Man with Razor at His Wrist
he's just a trope. Say, *Hey, buddy, tropes
are deathless. Don't give up on me now!*

Up side? I'm never out of work.
Just last week on *Law and Order,* I suicided
unironically in a posh Miami Beach salon.
Such banal blasphemy. My kingdom

for a trope curled around its own neck.
For trope-shears. For a hairdryer and a full
bathtub. For a pyre made of all the masks
I've worn for you. For a match. For a fistful

of fairy dust thrown onto the fire. For this
exeunt to exit. To mean as much alive
as I do dead.

Jan Becker

Summer at Jesus Camp (for Donna)

We were the only two campers
who called home and asked to stay another week.
Youandme weweresotight.
Maybe together was our home then.
That summer,
you crammed 87 pieces of popcorn in your cheeks
and I tried to touch Tom's dick
when we played Capture the Flag.
We spent hours tying lanyards in the art hut
with Becky, who couldn't ride horses,
because she'd broken her neck.
Every afternoon, we took a canoe out
on the lake. We tipped it over so many times,
they told us to stay on shore. I passed out
the day we climbed Mt. Greylock,
the world went white, and I heard some guy yell
out, "Jesus, she's passed out," as the ground swelled up and caught me.
I was thinking, Jesus,
maybe Melville did see Moby Dick up there.
We never made it to the summit.
Never reached an altitude of ambiguity.

I'd been sleepwalking the night before
on the shore of the lake
and the moon and the mountain had fallen into the water.
I was dreaming of spinning cartwheels like Leona,
and hiding under the rosebushes with the rattlesnakes
and you found me. You walked me back to my bunk
and tucked me in safe. You always tucked me in.

That day I passed out on the mountain,
Youandme, we were sleeping

under the eaves in the cabin
after the nurse sent me back to my bunk until dinner,
and you leaned over and asked me
Will Jesus still love me if I'm a lesbian?
I told you yeah.

I didn't know much of anything yet,
But I'd already learned everything I'd need.
I knew the answer before you even asked.
I was so poor that year, the pastor paid my way to camp
because I memorized I Corinthians 13.
(I never told him I thought Paul was mostly full of shit,
except for that chapter.)
I told you yeah.
We didn't speak in tongues of men or of angels.
All we knew that summer
was love.

Jason Schneiderman

The Buffy Sestina

The First Episode of the New Season, Before the Opening Credits.

Buffy is upstairs sharpening her large collection of stakes
when her mother comes upstairs and says, "Would it be bad,
just this once, not to go out staking vampires again tonight?"
After all — she had just defeated an apocalyptic force! Time
for a break? Buffy never has time for a break. Angel gone,
her stakes sharp, she kisses her mom and hops out the window

into the backyard. Buffy is familiar with this small window
at the beginning of every season (school year), when her stakes
are enough to fight her battles, and whatever the big coming
evil will be — it hasn't started to build yet. What big bad
will it be this season? She pulls her coat against the night
and there's Willow! Her best friend! She certainly has time

for Willow! They walk, explicate the summer, say, "Time
to go back to school." Suddenly, a vampire seizes this window
of relaxed defenses, and grabs off-guard Willow. Oh this night-
ly threat! Willow screams and resists. Buffy turns, her stake
at the ready. "Meet my friend, Mr. Pointy!" she says. Bad
bloodsucker, he lets Willow go. He wants to fight. He goes

at Buffy with everything, and Buffy (blue coat, boots) comes
back at him hard. The fight is oddly even. For a long time
(40 seconds, say), he gets in good blows. He hurts her bad,
she looks finished. She isn't getting back up again. A doe
leaps into the cemetery. All are distracted. Willow makes a stake
from a broken bench piece and the vampire tries to run into the night.

But Xander arrives, blocks the exit with his own stake. This night
is going terribly now (for the vampire)! The vampire goes
around to a crypt and tries to run inside, but it takes time

to pry open the gates. Too much time; Xander almost stakes
the vamp, but he stops to quip, and the effort goes bad.
The vampire throws him hard into the boarded-up window

of the crypt. Willow runs over, pulls a board from the window
for a new stake. Buffy's back up. Oh, what a luxury this night
is! Forever to fight just one, lone vampire. Xander's bad-
inage soundtracks the fight. Willow lunges and misses, coming
close, but too far left. Buffy kicks the vampire in the face, stake
brandished. He goes down, and she's on top of him this time.

Buffy stakes the vampire. He's dust. Whew! Wait. Bad. Crypts
don't have windows. The night is heavy and dark. That took a long time!
What's coming begins to come. Let's unboard that window.

Jason Schneiderman

Pornography II: The Capacity to Love

These naked girls really love animals
in ways that I just don't. My therapist
thinks it's because I never had pets
growing up. These naked girls must have
had pets, but not clothes. That's how
they grew up with the capacity for animal love
in the buff. I only grew up with the capacity
for didacticism and fear, bitterness,
the ability to judge myself by what I can't do.

Like what that girl is doing with a donkey —
I couldn't do that. I'm not flexible enough
or dedicated enough. My therapist wants me
to work things out with my Dad, but really,
I think I need the unconditional love of a dog
or monkey. I think that's what would set me
on the right path. Did these girls have weird
displaced Oedipal complexes that they somehow
brought to their afterschool job at the stable?

I'm sorry, women have Elektra complexes.
I'm the one who couldn't get it Oedipal.
If I had managed an Oedipal complex,
I would get to be straight, but gay as I am,
I'm not gay enough to take a donkey-cock

like that. My therapist says I'm a narcissist,
and I guess it's true, because that girl's
fucking a donkey and all I can talk about
is myself.

Jason Schneiderman

Pornography IV

When someone says,
"I'm going to take out

my dentures; I think
you'll like it," it doesn't

mean something has
gone wrong, or that

you made a poor
decision somewhere.

It's not in your catalog
of possibilities, because

it doesn't film well,
so you've never seen it,

but he's right,
you'll like it.

Jen Benka

Begin

non-sight seeing

in the dream the horizon line was vertical

god was an understandable urge

real religion was beside her body

tenderness re-enacting solitude

**

a few simple facts counteract desolation

restlessness is essential

manufactured debates are art-less

the joke depends on its delivery

a text can fail

"goodbye" works

**

the hypothesis is that under capitalism influencers are suspect

I am tired of your face on the internet

**

Antonio tells Carol and me that Michael is HIV positive and homeless

sometimes poetry is a reminder of helplessness

the graffiti reads "RIP 80's revolution"

**

she won't put the baby down or cut his hair or let him have anything plastic

she will teach him the difference between art and vandalism

**

A man from Texas leaves me voice mail. He never says his name, he just launches into what he explains is an original poem he has written especially for me. He shouts a few lines about daffodils and buzzing bees. Then he tries to guess my age and makes comments about my appearance. Abruptly, he hangs up.

I want to be friends with more women.

**

the silence underneath everything you're saying

the inaccessible source showing

your consideration of landscape

and opaque truth

the literary form of your legs

"open and affirming"

a poem that looks out not at

Jen Benka

For Muriel

One of the first books of poetry I owned was a paperback edition of *Immortal Poems of the English Language*. The promotional copy in the front of the book read:

TO LOVE,
TO SUFFER,
TO THINK …
is to seek poetry.

I imagine the lines spoken slowly in a deep man's voice over a public address system. I am Winston.

I bought the book in 1984 for a high school English class taught by an intimidating woman, Dr. D. It was widely whispered that Dr. D, with her cashmere sweater sets and perfectly pressed A-line skirts, was a lesbian and the companion of Dr. S, the guidance counselor, who was a dead-ringer for Gertrude Stein.

"Lift up your face, my love, lift up your mouth/ Kiss me and come to bed."[1]

I didn't fully understand the whispering, only that Dr. D and Dr. S had each other instead of men, which was deviant. Not living in a city, there wasn't much information about gay and lesbian life beyond some mentions in newspapers at the time about a "gay disease." By 1984, 1,800 people had died of AIDS. The majority of information back then about homosexuality was contained in the library, and accessing it required the card catalog and the courage to potentially be caught and labeled a pervert.

Big Brother is watching you.

"… Never to despise/ the homosexual who goes building another/ with touch with touch (not to despise any touch)/ each like himself, like herself each./ You are this.[2]

Dr. S passed away recently and in her obituary Dr. D described how they loved to travel, spending several summers in Africa, and others touring the U.S in their motor home.

Immortal Poems of the English Language was originally published in 1952 and reprinted in 1983. The book claimed to be "the most inclusive anthology of verse ever published at so low a price." Of the 150 "British and American masters" represented in the book, only ten were women, and by 1984, only six or seven of the poets were still living.

I didn't know how to look for you until I learned I was looking.

"Nobody suspects that there are living artists and living poets. All are dead: the musicians, the poets, the sculptors. This is a world of business. Reality is the city. Real men go to The Office."[3]

We studied Keats' poem, "Ode on a Grecian Urn." I drew little stars by the line, "Beauty is truth, truth beauty," but in the margin I wrote, "The urn is cold and has no emotion. Is this really a vessel for beauty?"

Ode to a Moment that Reveals Ugliness

Readying himself for his weekly radio address and not realizing the microphone was on, President Reagan said, "My fellow Americans, I'm pleased to tell you today that I've signed legislation that will outlaw Russia forever. We begin bombing in five minutes."

Ode to Never Better Late

For years, President Reagan refused to address the AIDS epidemic. When he finally did in 1987, close to 21,000 people had died from the disease.

"Flower flower flower flower/ Today for the sake of all the dead Burst into Flower."[4]

There is one history that is offered to us. It is not our history.

In 1988, I cut off all my hair and bought steel-toe boots. At a reception after a reading by Allen Ginsberg and William Burroughs, I asked Burroughs if he would sign my copy of *Naked Lunch*. He looked me in the eye and slurred, "You should get out of this shit-hole, boy."

To be found out.

I asked my college English professor when we might read some women poets who weren't gassed and missing. He recommended that I read Adrienne Rich's work. I don't remember where in Rich's work it was that she mentioned the poet Muriel Rukeyser, but I wrote the name down.

Yes, our eyes saw each other's eyes
Yes, our mouths saw each other's mouths
Yes, our breasts saw each other's breasts
Yes, our bodies entire saw each other
Yes, it was beginning in each
Yes, it threw waves across our lives[5]

To find.

If we were not isolated, if we could recognize each other, if we knew the stories of our successes, if we refused their lies, we might know our power.

I touch her cheek. You are this. Kiss me. Flower flower. Come to bed.

"They fear it. They turn away, hand up palm out/ fending off moment of proof, the straight look, poem."[6]

Lying in the middle of Fifth Avenue in front of St. Patrick's Cathedral, Bill started yelling SHAME and soon we were all yelling SHAME SHAME SHAME. It was the 25th anniversary of the Stonewall Riots. Christopher was sick. And the sand was pouring out. And we were the sand and you were not the sand. SHAME.

"You will enter the world which eats itself"[7]

And it was and it is. Feeding on its own flesh. This is what it feels like to suffocate. To collapse from the inside out. Where is the glass to break. The stop to pull. Cut Cut.

If communication has broken down, then it is time to tap the roots of communication. Poetry is written from these depths; in great poetry you feel a source speaking to another source. And it is deep at these levels that the questions lie. They come up again and again during these years, when under all the surface shouting, there is silence about those things we need to hear.[8]

On February 21, 1995, Christopher Fons died at the age of 27. His brother Dan said, "When Christopher was in the room, I felt ten times stronger—stronger in my ability and in my determination to fight injustice. Christopher... lived true to his convictions every minute of every day, whether that meant passing out condoms to high school students in front of irate parents or the simple and profound act of holding hands with his boyfriend at a bus stop."[9]

The faces of the sufferers
in the street, in dailiness,
their lives showing
through their bodies
a look as of music
the revolutionary look
that says I am in the world
to change the world
my lifetime
is to love to endure to suffer the music
to set its portrait
up as a sheet of the world
the most moving the most alive[10]

At Christopher's funeral, and at his, at his, at his, at his and his. Circling around women with our arms linked, escorting them into the abortion clinic. Collecting knives from the men waiting to get into the shelter for the night. Watching the crack house burn. The bombing begins in five minutes.

Choose your poet here. Or, rather, do not choose. But remember what happened to you when you came to your poem, any poem whose truth overcame all inertia in you at that moment, so that your slow mortality took its proper place, and before it the light of a new awareness was not something new, but something you *recognized*.[11]

Notes:

1. "Drunken Girl," *Beast in View,* Muriel Rukseyser, 1944
2. "Despisals," *Breaking Open,* Rukeyser, 1973
3. *The Life of Poetry,* Rukeyser, (Reprinted by Paris Press, 1996)
4. "The Power of Suicide," *The Speed of Darkness,* Rukeyser, 1968
5. "Looking at Each Other," *Breaking Open,* Rukeyser, 1973
6. "Reading Time: 1 Minute 26 Seconds," *A Turning Wind,* Rukeyser, 1939
7. "Nine Poems: for the unborn child," *The Green Wave,* Rukeyser, 1948
8. *The Life of Poetry,* Rukeyser, (Reprinted by Paris Press, 1996)
9. "History of Gay and Lesbian Life in Milwaukee, Wisconsin"
10. "Kathe Kollwitz," *The Speed of Darkness,* Rukeyser, 1968
11. *The Life of Poetry,* Rukeyser, (Reprinted by Paris Press, 1996)

Jericho Brown

A.D.

Each wounds you badly, but no boy hurts
Like the first one did

When you slept in a bed
Too narrow for two. You thought he disappeared

In the sheet and cushion,
But look at you now, 28 in a king, you wake

With a man on your mind — Head
On your chest, both of you bent

As best you can to make
Room for the other.

Ten years, your feet hanging, tangled and long, and still
You're the victim

Of such nightmares. You breathe
Like he's been lying

On top for the last decade.
A man dies above you, you suffocate below the weight.

Jericho Brown

Layover

Dallas is so far away
Even for the people who live
In Dallas is Dallas far away
A hub
Through which we get
To smaller places
That lurch and hurt
Mean stopping
In Dallas and all are
From small towns and farms
If all keep going
Back far enough
Pay attention
Keep your belongings near
Everyone in Dallas
Is still driving
At 3:24 a.m. off I-20
Where I was raped
Though no one
Would call it that
He was inside
By the time I realized
He thought it necessary
To leave me with knowledge
I can be hated
I was smaller then
One road went through me
No airport
I drove him home
There had been a wreck

On the interstate
I sat in traffic
My wallet on the seat
In between my legs.

Jericho Brown

To Be Asked for a Kiss

Suicide's Note
by Langston Hughes
The calm,
Cool face of the river
Asked me for a kiss.

The desire to be dead and the desire not to be alive and the desire to kill oneself are three different desires.

The desire to die is not the desire to be dead. Anyone who has ever been in love knows this.

And though all of these desires seem — to those who have never had them — synonymous with the desire to run away, they are not the desire to run away. Any look at the recent statistics on gay teen suicide is proof of this.

I am, because I've been assigned to think in this way about this poem, trying to remember the last time I wanted to kill myself. I don't have to remember the last time I wanted to die because that would be as simple as remembering the last time I had sex without a condom.

When people ask me to examine a poem I love, they mean for me to dismantle the poem … to undress the one I love before them down to his linebreaks, his rhythms, his slick and sustained use of metaphor. They want to know why I love and how they should. They want love coming out of my mouth to be more mathematical than it is in their own lives.

"Suicide's Note" is one sentence long. Counting its title, the poem is 14 words, 17 syllables, a single tercet.

Here, an audience would like for me to say a thing or two about haiku and its relationship to the blues stanza, but I'll get to that later. Maybe.

Langston Hughes published "Suicide's Note" in his first book, *The Weary Blues,* in 1926, which means he was less than 24 years old when he wrote it.

I don't know whether or not Hughes ever considered suicide, and of course, I don't think that matters.

Or do I?

I believe it matters that Langston Hughes was careful not to do anything to make us perceive him as someone capable of a negative thought. And so a star is born. And so black folk know the name of at least one black poet.

But none of that is my assignment.

I am to examine a poem I love. And examine means that you want, at least, to know what I think of the title.

"Suicide" is both a verb and a noun. The title of the poem and the lack of an article before the word "suicide" allows us to begin to think of the act as a being, a personage capable of writing something as thoughtful as a note.

If I had committed suicide when I was 12 or 14 or 16 or 18 or 20 or 22, I would not have left a note.

Now I remember. I was 22. Look at what writing can do. It can help me remember and to smile at Sexton's "unnameable lust return[ing]" to me every other year for ten years.

Where was I?

The note.

The joy I had in thinking of how best to get rid of myself was always tied to inventing ways for it to seem an accident. *What time is the bus that's on time when I'm late and rushing across the street? Do I know anyone on the roof of a building I can help? How many pain pills is an accident?*

I would not have left a note because the suicide is — believe it or not — the most competitive person in the world. I once understood death as a competition. I had to do it before anyone or anything else did it to me. I was interested in winning, and I was convinced that someone would interpret a note left behind as a letter of surrender.

The first line of the poem is end-stopped, marking the beginning of the speaker's end. The break after "the calm" — such a truncated phrase — calls again to our understanding of a single word with two functions. If the title of the poem shows us some embodiment of the act of suicide, then the first line defines its outcome as "calm."

Whenever I read a poem, I read for what it doesn't say. In the church where I was raised, one of the things for which so many people publicly prayed every Sunday is peace. The calm of the suicide, like his note, is the dream of the speaker, the self he is after, the self that is not there.

Alliteration starts the second line, and we begin to understand "calm" more fully as an adjective and not only a noun.

Here comes the blues I was supposed to play earlier.

While the poem is not a blues poem in its form exactly, the second line fully positions it as a blues poem in its content. As in haiku, the blues stanza juxtaposes two seemingly different images or ideas or emotions in order to show the interrelatedness of the two.

In his 1926 essay, "The Negro Artist and the Racial Mountain," Hughes calls the blues, "incongruous humor that so often … becomes ironic laughter mixed with tears."

What is a "cool face?" If it is a face that expresses disapproval or the aloof nature of its owner, don't we wonder why she is so mean and how we can please her? If it is a face in full confidence of its beauty or with features that attract us, don't we want that face to look our way?

The alliteration of "calm" and "cool" in this poem ties me to its pull down toward its final piece of punctuation. And "the river" means to make that movement downward toward the end all the more gentle. Water quenches thirst. Water flows free.

Langston Hughes wrote what is probably his most famous poem, "The Negro Speaks of Rivers" when he was 18 years old.

He wrote about rivers until the end of his life. In some of the poems, they are sites for murder. In others, they are sites for suicide.

In Hughes's poems where rivers are sites for suicide, the speaker is the victim of unrequited love.

Yes, we could drown in a river, but we could also drown in someone's loving arms. Now doesn't that sound like the blues?

The act of suicide as a personage is, in this poem, one with the river. It flows in one direction.

I don't know why I stopped wanting to kill myself. I didn't have a therapist. I didn't take medication. I imagine I am the last of those raised by binary believers. To us, it was told that white people had few troubles, and they couldn't deal with any of them without another bill to pay for anti-depressants or for someone to listen.

I am old enough to be of a generation of black people who didn't think black people killed themselves. Adults would say as much.

When my lover cries about a black boy as far away from us as Johnson & Wales University in Providence, Rhode Island, hanging himself in his dorm room, my lover cries because nothing we heard adults say while we were young seems true.

Forty-three percent of black gay teens have contemplated or attempted suicide. My lover has never been to Rhode Island.

Alliteration moves to consonance and then back again to alliteration in the final line of the poem. Only now, the sound we've encountered by way of the letter "c" comes to us through the more definite letter "k."

Africa. Afrika. Clan. Klan.

"K" is the first letter in the word "kindness."

Suicide — "the calm, cool face of the river" — was kind enough to have "asked" the speaker. And for what?

Whenever I read a poem, I read for what it doesn't say. The speaker — and this has a great deal to do with why I love this poem so much — is dead. He talks to me, to us, from the grave.

Even from the grave, he admits that all he ever wanted was to be asked for a kiss.

"Suicide's Note" is not a poem about suicide. On the contrary, it is a poem about living forever. About finally getting what we want and getting it even after death.

The poem is interested in the immortality of poetry. The speaker doesn't want to die as much as he wants to oblige. Who doesn't want a kiss? Who doesn't want a cool face to ask for that kiss?

I don't remember why I stopped wanting to kill myself, but I do know how I stay alive. Though I love to kiss my lover, it is not because of his kisses. Though I am laid open when he cries, it is not because of his tears.

I live to write poems. And I write poems because it's all I can do to stave off death, or as Sexton said before killing herself, "Suicide is, after all, the opposite of the poem." After all.

Only poems allow me the opportunity, even when I get them wrong, to try at communicating with the dead and, hopefully, with those who have yet to live.

By the time I turned 22, I don't know that I wanted to stay alive, but I did, and still do, want to write a poem.

Jim Elledge

Zigzag *adv.* [<Ger. *zacke,* a tooth, sharp prong, or point]

The spring just after he turns seven, H picks his nose until it bleeds and slips out of his father's apartment through the front door, its only door. He spends whole nights with a warehouse night watchman downtown. They play a game with the flashlight the night watchman invented. He tells H he's the best player ever, so much better than all the other boys rolled into one, so long-lasting, so agile! H never tells anyone. Not a word. Not an adult. Nobody ever catches them. Not a soul. Not an adult. But later, when they send him away to the Asylum, he'll teach others, who'll giggle and giggle, too, during the game. It doesn't have a single rule, only a surprise at the end.

Jim Elledge

Umpire *vt.* [<M.Fr. *nomper* a third person]

I take. You take. He, she, it takes. We take. You take. They take. They take. They do take. They. They took. They take. They will take because they've taken. They. They do. And that's where H begins at every blue moon. Snatch, make off with, lift, ransack, crib, cop, pinch, nip, snitch, he continues, and it doesn't stop there, that urge to build a bridge between the past and the present, the present and the future; the need to forge a chain where only twine had been; the hunger to collect, to hoard, to stack. His recitation is litany, penitence, and sanctuary in equal parts, blood's tide throbbing throughout his body. Nick, mooch, mug, snare, pilfer, filch, rob, burgle, pickpocket, stick up. This isn't a game. The list he concocts relieves the pressure that builds behind his eyes. That's what he tells himself when he catches himself stuttering the list he created and confined to memory so many years ago now that he doesn't recollect the details — only the relief. Steal, thieve, purloin, swipe, appropriate, palm, highjack, plunder, pillage. Loot, sack, fleece, maraud, pirate, shanghai, abscond with, kidnap. Kidnap. Kidnap. They do. They have. That's where he stops, where the list ends — like a rosary's decades—at its beginning. He can catch his breath there. He can cat nap. He can dream Whillie alive again and beside him at Riverview or Elsie safe in her mother's arms. That's where the pressure's gone at last, the blood's calm, and the haunting's over — until the next time.

Jim Elledge

Hubbub *n.* [<Celt. *ubub,* exclamation of aversion]

Almost cordial is H these days, the mature adult, minding his Ps and Qs, not like hell-bent, I-addicted sissy-boy H, who cruised West Madison, luring drunks into alleys with promises he sometimes even kept while stealing their money, who threw (not drew) bricks at bullies, who slashed his teacher's face with a knife. The burlesque houses made promises: their blaring ragtime, their women and drag queens glittering, slinging their diaphanous silks and bright satins into circles, the circles swirling into tornadoes. All the men deftly, furtively adjusted themselves. H saw them. He watched *for* them. He dreamt *of* them lined up in a chorus line ready, eager, willing. But these days a calmer H holds up at home in a corner of his room thumbing through coloring books or the funnies, looking for pictures of little girls and boys to trace or transcribing into a Penworthy notebook the litany The Unseen intones from the tree outside his window. The words are nearly unreadable, his hands shake so much.

Jim Elledge

Burlesque *adj.* [<It. *burlesco* <*buria,* a jest, mockery]

H's daddy, a German tailor, taught H how to read newspapers before he even went to school, how to sew with a tiny needle, how to measure a man's inside leg with a tape, asking, on his knees looking up and in perfect American English, "On which side do you lay, sir?" through straight pins between his lips. H traces (not faces) little girls and boys from coloring books, newspaper ads, and circulars, then erases (not embraces) their clothing, a striptease so clean not a soul gets bruised. Winds gusting from H's pencil snatch off their blouses and skirts. Tornadoes rise from his pen as he draws penises on them freehand. Weather is the key to H's strategy: It's so much easier arriving at the naked truth when you storm across whatever lines have been strung in your way.

Jim Elledge

Algebra *n.* [<Ar. *al-jabr,* the reunion of broken parts]

What a sumptuous vaudeville the alphabet of H's grief is! He lines it up in a row from dainty Z to lazy M to loudmouthed A: part soliloquy, part wisecrack, part penitence. He recites it late at night in varying voices, a solitary, if multi-talented, barker to his own theatrics. You might think his hi-jinks a kooky cabaret, even a striptease for eggheads: one cadence after another slipped off and tossed beyond the spotlight and falling lazily to the stage as he gyrates to a bump-and-grind as uniquely H's as his finger prints. Note in his paintings all those insides spilled outside, all those hands and feet nailed to crossbeams, posts, and trees, all those tongues thrust out and vibrating, soundless never thoughtless. Grammar and syntax, that's what H's all about — a linguistics of watercolor and crayons, of tracings and piles of magazines and coloring books. You can hear it clear as can be, if you don't let the screams from the butchery get in the way.

a dolphin dies
being passed a
round for selfies
is some
thing still
a
live here
no
its dead we
are dead
our
blow
hole stuf
fed
with sand our sk
in palm
slapped
mass
aged
and
passed
a
round
for baby

this is here our
face

this the hu
man heart
made
fish for some
one else

to fry
made
read
y for
the
thud
in
side
the con
cave
grave of
hu
man hu
man hu
man going
down the
drain

its true

from
here
it *can*
all look
the
same
but
that's
just an
ill
usion
—a
trick

the light
plays on
    the dry
    ing
    eye of
    death..
delight.

this
dream
    is
    what it
    looks like:
    a
    broke
    n leg a
    sea shell
    knife
    cutting
    the fat,

our
    floating face
our
poor reced
    ing wave
our
    lit
    tle close
        up
    made in
    china

and yes, we scream
    of course,
we scream
    'cause
its our moment

and whatever
    can be
    said
is just a sad
campaign
a virtue signal
from beyond the planet
Posture

all of this
of course
    could
    be
    our lit
    tle
secret
but we
    just love
secreting
    love
to tell
the world
    to
    smile
knowing

the hu
man brain
            is but
the hu
man
heart
            is just a
            maw

so may
            be
            just
warm up
            whatever
sand you
 can around
                        you

may
be just
shut up
and

maybe just
shut up

maybe just
shut up

and
smile

José A. Villar-Portela

A Life in Heels

You arrive. Lymph nodes clogged,
fresh from the market deli, a boy
-senberry beauty in a bathrobe
singing Self and Body sleep, singing

you

are verb made slow, a film
spread thin over the droning
lens of World so Slant & Skew can
slut their way around The Real, do

what they came to do: distort, destroy,
cut every brick called Home into
a line and snort the body homeless.

Undone, unhinged & uninvited, you've
nonetheless
arrived. The party's
not for you, but you know how
to blow out each and every candle. When someone
asks to keep watch over
the cake, swat summer flies
away, you gorge instead
on every piece of sugarmeat
ever denied you,
wake up from diabetic
dreams a decade down the line, climb
down your own braid to the suburbs—
is this Oz or Hialeah Hospital, freedom or
just a high

fever? It is your quinceañera, after all,
and you're

arriving. You're
still deranged in
business suits & manic swirling
for the pearl, an ultra-wristed
infra-fairy fuck dressed up in pastel
pasties for the prom.

But look, no hands;
look, Mom, no Self,
just every brick
called Home being carried out
onto the dance floor
of another life: a life
in heels, a fever *and*
a freedom.

Joseph O. Legaspi

Revelation

> Harper: … This is the very threshold of revelation sometimes.
> You can see things … Do you see anything about me?
>
> Prior: Yes.
> — Tony Kushner,
> *Angels in America: Millennium Approaches*

His moon-white torso flashes like strobe lights
in the club where we met last night as the subway stalls
on 42nd Street, *the crossroads of the world* sings the disembodied
voice of the morning conductor.
        I return to carnal acts performed
in darkness: kisses plump as crushed tomatoes,
my lover and I were ravenous, partaking on the harvest
of our nipples' rosy bulbs, tearing at our limbs like meats
on a medieval table. Our tongues snakecharmed goosebumps
to the surface of our flesh. His weight pressing
against me drove me ecstatic to asphyxiation.
He Anglosaxoned me, the divinity of his
England flooded my mouth with light.
        A conundrum this union
of identical bodies, fusing in hungry, irrational
ways, squeezing a camel through a needle's eye:
a defiance of nature, which is nature.
        I didn't know the man,
we were foreigners sharing a language
spoken incongruently — lilts, crests, pitches.
But I tread familiar territory like my childhood
tropics. I was sherpa to my terrains
of Asia, yes, the entire continent
for I had grown immense.
        At dawn, with his fingers the British
boy feathered the slope of my back,

the blue light softening his face,
and the world outside escaped.
  We entered a threshold of revelation,
ether of lucidity, truth telling. I asked,

When you look at me, what do you see?
He said, *A homosexual.*

As he fell asleep, I watched the stranger,
the sour breathing of his gentle wellspring.
Where were the prophetic, wrathful angels?
  I then realized I am not afraid of men,
nor the masculine hyperbole of men who love men,
and my father was not in that hotel room.
  I felt the archipelagic islands had gathered—
a wholeness like Pangaea, when Earth was young,
its landmass unimaginably one.

Joseph O. Legaspi

Whom You Love

"Tell me whom you love, and I'll tell you who you are."
— Creole Proverb

The man whose throat blossoms with spicy chocolates

Tempers my ways of flurrying

Is my inner recesses surfacing

Paints the bedroom blue because he wants to carry me to the skies

Pear eater in the orchard

Whitmanesque in his urges & urgencies

My Bear, the room turns orchestral

Crooked grin of ice cream persuasion

When I speak he bursts into seeds & religion

Poetry housed in a harmonica

Line dances with his awkward flair

Rare steaks, onion rings, Maker's on the rocks

Once-a-boy pilfering grenadine

Nebraska, Nebraska, Nebraska

Wicked at the door of happiness

At a longed-for distance remains sharply crystalline

Fragments, but by day's end assembled into joint narrative

Does not make me who I am, entirely

Heart like a fig, sliced

Peonies in a clear round vase, singing

A wisp, a gasp, sonorous stutter

Tuning fork deep in my belly, which is also a bell

Evening where there is no church but fire

Sparks, particles, chrysalis into memory

Moth, pod of enormous pleasure, fluttering about on a train

He knows I don't need saving & rescues me anyhow

Our often-misunderstood kind of love is dangerous

Darling, fill my cup; the dove has come to roost

Joseph O. Legaspi

Rouge

From her floral make-up purse my mother
has fished out, flipped open her seashell
compact, the rabbit tail brush dabbed
with pressed powder sweeps across my
face, feathering into alabaster, a masking.

Throughout my grade school performances—
whether stuffed inside a tomato costume or
sandwiched between cardboards to resemble
a book—my mother has applied foundation,
blush, talcum, highlighting mascara, to conceal
and reveal: boy and actor, flesh and porcelain.

Backstage, her slender finger glides her lipstick
red on my lips, pearly puckered. She's leaning so
close we're exchanging breaths. Transference
from a woman who never leaves the house
without her face impeccably drawn, hair
fashionably in a bun. Who, during the heat
of equatorial afternoons, locks her children
in her bedroom for *siesta* to preserve our light

skin. I am learning beauty, I am learning to be
feminine, and shoulder the cruelties accorded
a boy with flair. I put forth face of even tone,
void of harshness. What a beautiful mother
does to her son. Escorting him to the stage.

With the taste of petrolatum in my mouth,
hair slicked back with pomade, crowned
with a poinsettia head dress, I'm in the garden
of a Christmas pageant, perfumed, armored

with memorized rhyming lines and conspicuous anonymity among bare-faced classmates. Before a cat-eyed audience I flower, glowing in make-shift health, rouge like smolder of the cheeks.

JP Howard

A Love Letter to The Decades I have Kissed or Notes on Turning 50

Dear 10-year-old Juliet,
remember Mama wouldn't let anyone,
not even your favorite dance teacher, Mrs. Carter, shorten your name.
Mama said, *No abbreviations of Juliet's name are permitted.*
Thank you very much.

I loved when Mrs. Carter called me *Jewels*
(that's how I imagined she spelled it, J-E-W-E-L-S,
a glittering diamond of a word
in her mouth, *Demi-plié* or *pirouette Jewels*).
I would turn, twirl, pale pink leotards floating across the room.
When Mama left the room, Mrs. C would whisper in MY ear,
Jewels keep making magic child.
Kiss the dance teacher who made your name a precious stone.

Dear 20-year-old JP,
remember the hippie poet from California
who came to Barnard for a poetry reading your sophomore year,
and seduced you with her smooth poet words.
She whispered in your ear one night,
When you graduate come to me.
Remember HOW you showed up at her doorstep in San Francisco;
the look of shock on her face.
She felt bad, all those miles you traveled,
and let you stay in her apartment that summer,
while she moved in with her girlfriend.
Remember HOW you fell in love with San Francisco,
the Castro, those women's bars and bathhouses,
35-year old Tosca, scent of her leather jacket
ripping through you as you rode towards Twin Peaks
on the back of her Harley.
Janet Jackson and the Pleasure Principle on full blast.
Kiss the poet who left her doors open for you that summer.

Dear 30-year-old playa, playa JP
Remember all the exes you invited to your 30th birthday bash?
Only a Leo would do this crazy shit, your best friend teased.
Remember the drama, how you craved it. The women, how you craved them.
Some nights two, three at a time.
We only live once, you told yourself.
Remember the lover who finally said,
You can't have me and all these women too.
I want you, but I don't want to share you.
Remember how much you loved her, how much you wanted it to work,
how scared you were of your decade-old patterns.
Kiss the lover who stayed, especially when you were scared she would leave.

Dear 40-year-old Juliet Pearl,
remember you tried so hard to have a second child?
You didn't want your first born to be the fourth generation
of only children in your tiny little family.
Remember your lovers' hands, gently helping you guide the needle,
the fertility treatments, the look of worry on her face after the last IVF.
Remember the surprise party your lover gave you on your 40th birthday,
belly round with promise of baby.
Kiss your lover who stayed by your side for a decade.

Dear 50-year-old JP poet,
Remember the last decade. And decades that came before.
Giving birth at forty, then your MFA a few years later. And all those poems.
Celebrate your lover. She is still here. Two decades into this relationship.
20 and 30-year-old Juliet would have never guessed this could happen.
Remember ups, then downs. That rare illness that almost took your lover.
Remember your boys growing up like beams of light. Black boys shining.
Circle of love growing. Poems everywhere.
Kiss your reflection in the mirror. Celebrate her. Write her a love poem.

JP Howard

149th Street, Sugar Hill, Harlem

When I was seven, I had my first crush on my best friend Yvette,
who adults all said looked like a young Lena Horne,
all I know is she was pretty and liked to play dress up with my Barbie dolls.
Mama was tough and smart.
When Peanut's cousin, who everybody said got high all the time,
robbed Mama and me in our elevator,
Mama yelled "Muthafucka just take the money!"
He didn't even realize Mama made sure to take her keys out her little purse,
before turning it over.
I didn't ride elevators again for ten more years.
Our scraggly gray poodle Squeak-Squeak didn't even bark.
Mama said he was a little good-for-nothing pet, but I still loved him.
When me and Tiffany dropped water balloons
from my third floor apartment on our crotchety neighbor Mrs. Long,
Ms. Janet told on us and we both got our butts beat that summer.
It was worth watching old Mrs. Long's wig fall off her shiny bald head.
When folks started calling our neighborhood Hamilton Heights
we all said that sound too fancy.
Anyhow, when summer heat gets too hot for our tiny apartments,
old men still pull out their folding chairs and sit on the stoop.
We still Sugar Hill.

JP Howard

M A R K it UP

if this poem could talk she would **S C R E A M:**

muthafuka don't write me in no fuckin form
don't write me in haiku, cinqku, sonnet or that tercet shyt
please whateva you do **DON'T TRY & SOUNDMEOUT!**
Let me ramble onandonandon................ get alla this anger out let me
spread my stuff all over the page
do not hem me in between some fancy ass words

let me enter the room on my terms

if you must push me up on
some syllables don't let those
suckas rhyme leave that for
all those fancy forms that

drop in journals. i've got my own style

RESPECT!!!

if this poem could talk she would
wrap herself around your throat
burn as you swallow her whole
tag your vocal chords with blood red spray paint:

SHE WAS HERE.

JP Howard

i am

i am dyke bulldagger lesbo femme butch lipstick lesbianboi lez gay queer aggressive androgynous soft butch femagress lezzie bulldyke diesel dyke baby dyke stealth dyke drag dyke bear dyke trans dyke spiritual stud soft boi bean flicker carpet muncher muff diver   pussy puncher todger dodger lesbian homo pungent scent hard nippled loud moan soft nibble tongue nape of neck   whispered earlobe pulled loc melted dark/milk/white chocolate wet lipped cocoa butter round rubbed tattooed back sweet ass ready to be rode spanked licked fucked pushed poet woman.

JP Howard

A Leo Love Letter to Myself

Dear Jewels,

I'm going to keep this short and sweet. I've been trying to get your attention for a long time. But between your day gig, parent-teacher conferences, kids basketball practices, poetry salons and stolen moments with your woman, well you get the point girl. Life has been ridiculously busy. I love that your life is better than those half-hearted childhood dreams. You were so short-sighted. Never dreamt your current life. Technicolor is so much better than monochrome. Who would've guessed that you found love and started a family, after all those women. Damn! They were sexy and fine as hell and cray cray! Remember that crazy bitch who returned all your panties to you on the conference table in the middle of a meeting at your first job? Didn't your mama teach you not to shit where you eat? And Tosca, the 31 year old diva who took you on her Harley to Twin Peaks when you were 19. San Francisco will always remind you of the smell of her leather jacket. Girlfriend, I agree with your life philosophy: a ménage a trios with two of your sexiest friends is something every lesbian must do before settling down. You might get some slack on that one, but I've got your back. And yes, girl what goes around comes around. You learned that shit the hard way. Anyhow, I'm trying to tell you something girlfriend. I love that you've taken all the shit life has dealt and lived to tell the story. I love you for being sexy and impatient and I think you've beat the world record for maintaining friendships with more of your ex's than can fit in this letter. What's that about anyway? Anyhow, I digress. This letter is much longer than I intended. But you are more complicated than I remember. I love you, you sexy motherfucker!

Love,
J

Julie Marie Wade

After Words

Imagine a Tuesday in early spring,
a purple sky puckered at the corners.

Maybe you are walking home from school,
just walking—small again, & with a flutter
in your throat for telling secrets.

And when you bend over suddenly
to pour the story inside her studded ear—

there is nothing,

suddenly, nothing

ii.

Imagine now how
she studies you, brown eyes
bordered by tortoise shell

And what you want to tell her
your gut aches from saving so long

(*Take them,* string of Sapphic breaths

until she passes,
her trim brows

raised)

iii.

Maybe you are only seven years old.
        Maybe you are still in kindergarten.

But even then, you were not without words,   not without

                                                            language

If you love her, say it—

        ring around ring around ring around the

If you love her, some annunciation   rosie   *is required*

Julie Marie Wade

Shooting Pool with Anne Heche the Day After Ellen & Portia's Wedding

For starters, the waiter was slow as fuck
bringing our beers, & Heche kept
clenching her tiny fist in her pink,
splayed palm & muttering,
"Somebody's about to get clobbered."

"Aw, you're just sore ..." I say, trailing off,
thinking about the backroom broadcast &
the white-on-white cover of *People* magazine.
Now she is snapping her gum & strutting
around this green velvet like she owns the place,
& I'm starting to feel that itch in my throat
that means both intrigue & fear.

"Go ahead," she says, "tell me something *terrible*
about myself," & rocks on her heels.

I could tell her how we call it "getting heched"
when a woman you like, or love, leaves you
for a man. I could explain that, unlike the tired
Uhaul jokes, she's still with us, fresh as a paper
cut that starts small, then seems to gnaw & gnaw.

But when I look at her, quick appraisal under
the low-hanging light — her tight, pale arms,
her compact body beneath the red ribbed tank top
& cut-off shorts, it's a feeling like not-quite-attraction
& not-quite-compassion, so I play it off with a wave:

I say: "Don't you know by now you're America's
favorite hasbian?" Yeah, I thought she would like that.

She takes a bow, & her taut green veins stand out everywhere, a stunning ovation. The adrenaline passes from her hand to the cue on a luge of newly focused intention.

"Goddamn right I am!" she grins. "Now watch me put this ball in that pocket."

Julie Marie Wade

Portrait of Tolerance as a Picket Fence

From a distance, they resembled spears poised for piercing,
& I thought of the bad nanny in *The Hand that Rocks the Cradle*,
how she drops to her demise from the widow's walk of a house
in North Tacoma, which was only about an hour from where I lived
at the time; & when she falls, the picket passes through her body
like a stake, the way people killed vampires before they knew any better;
& I thought of the TV show called *Picket Fences* that my parents
disapproved of after the dimly lit adolescent lesbian kiss, which was
only the second of such kisses ever to air on television by 1993, when
everyone was still concerned about the *gay gene* & proving that
homosexuals were not *obscene*, just "hormonally compelled toward
unnatural acts" only useful for boosting ratings during Sweeps Week
or striking flint to start a ruckus, to rally around, & eventually
to censor — in praise of the Greater Good. I didn't watch
Ellen's coming out in 1997. I was a senior in high school with my
head buried deep in a book of Frost's poetry, trying to live in the past,
hoping to hide from the world that might be waiting, but taken with the line
Before I built a wall, I'd ask to know what I was walling in or walling out.
And I had seen *Mr. Wrong* when it premiered the year before, thinking
maybe *he's* not the only thing wrong, maybe she's just not *drawn* to men
in the way that some women are. A fence, as far as I can tell, is
comparable to a wall, but with one compelling difference — it can be
seen through, as in I am looking at you as I am relegating you to your
corner, as I am cordoning off my property to please me &
my kind. *Stay on your side of the line.* Maybe, in the future,
we'll come up short a hand for bridge or poker, & One of Us with the
power to speak for all the others will shout out, *Red Rover, Red Rover,*
Send One of Them right over, & the barbecue will continue tediously
over all-beef franks & garden burgers, & someone will say, "I can't believe
you're gay, you seem so *normal*" — or something to that effect — & you'll play
along because you want to belong to the PTA or the Neighborhood Consortium

of Concerned Citizens. That night in your journal, you'll write: "The only thing wrong with difference is the different part." *Aside from that*, you'll say—
closing the gate, crossing the yard, counting like sheep the many *to whom you were likely to give offence*, & the few who knew better but chose not to raise
their hands.

Julie Marie Wade

Self-Portrait in Ugly Pants

The thing is, there were *a lot*
of ugly pants. You think
I'm kidding, but I'm not.
You think I'm exaggerating,
but you wouldn't be caught
living or dead in pants like these.
The Goodwill was less than pleased.
They wouldn't take most of them.

I had many a pair of high-water jeans.
They were mottled, with a low V
that dipped down at the waist,
an arrow pointing right to the crotch,
& pockets that pulled at the seams.
They were a denim chastity belt, those jeans.

I had khaki pants that were pleated in front
with fabric over the zipper that formed a lump
where a penis would be. When I sat down,
it filled out like a sack of balls. I was the best-
endowed girl in the fifth grade class. So glad.
My breasts hadn't come in yet, but my penis had.

There were culottes, too, which are part of the lottes
I mean when I say there were *lots* of ugly pants.
Polka dots & panty lines, a sacky ass
that drooped about like a basset hound's
deep set of sobering jowls. I'm surprised I
didn't howl when they bore the impression
of my bicycle seat. There is no lesson
that pants like these can learn.

Let us not forget the elastic band of
the grandma brand — Sag Harbor sweat pants
that can sack adolescent confidence faster than
most can say "Metamucil." Fortunately, for me,
my mom ironed the creases in good, so when
the pant legs shook, they looked like the sails
of a ship at sea. That ship should have
been christened *The USS Ugly.*

When I met the love of my life,
I was wearing navy blue dress slacks
two inches too short, & with the sewn-in
cuffs, make that five. But dead or alive,
I was going down in those clamdiggers,
I thought — over a cliff or into her arms.
Like a traumatized patient in a crowded ER,
we cut them off me & never looked back.

Julie R. Enszer

Pervert

The week before my mother died
I went to a feminist theory seminar,
and even though I can describe myself
as nothing other than happily married,
I wanted another woman.
An old school butch —
the kind of woman who exudes lesbian
through every pore of her being,
the kind of woman who sits comfortably
with her legs apart, who stands
forcefully, both feet firmly on the ground,
the kind of woman we describe
as ballsy and, on occasion, a ball-buster,
the kind of woman whose eyes
sear femmes's bodies,
making our nipples hard,
our clits erect,
our pussies wet —
the kind of woman I desire.
It was not just that I admired
her power, not just that I appreciated
her sexual being walking through the world,
glancing at me, giving me the benefit of lust.
No, I had to indulge
in the full-frontal fantasy.
During two days of seminars,
I imagined her fist hungrily
inserted in my vagina,
her long fingers first stroking
my muscular walls, gathering
the rhythm of sex, opening me
to accommodate four fingers,
a thumb, squeezed into a fist;

I imagined how my body
would open for her, how my lips
would quiver when my body erupted
into orgasm. I imagined looking into her eyes
as the ripples of my orgasm
squeezed her tight fist more deeply
into my body. I imagined making
her core to my body, central in my life,
in the way that only sex and lust bring
two women together. I imagined sucking her nipples,
laughing with her in the afterglow.
I imagined how much she would want
me after I took her whole hand
inside me, and, though I do not
believe this, when my father called
to tell me about the bleed
in my mother's brain and how
I needed to come home to help him
with the work death entails,
to mourn with him,
to bury my mother,
though I do not believe this at all,
I could not help but think:
I caused my mother's death
with my lust. Her death was G-d's
punishment for being an avowed
homosexual, punishment for my desire
of someone outside marriage,
for my continual, unrelenting lust for women,
which my mother had condemned
since I was eighteen.
I could not help but see my mother

in death somehow justified
in her anger, in her continued disappointment
with my perversity. I could not help but
think: I am a pervert who caused
my mother's death.
I could not help but hear
her final, fatal words, crushing
the lust, the fantasy from the conference.
She knew all along I would kill her,
after death she hissed,
I told you,
I told you so.

Julie R. Enszer

At the New York Marriage Bureau

We present passports —
federal documents — for a license
the nation will not recognize.

Outside rain is pouring
from cloudy skies. We marvel
at bureaucratic efficiency:

swipe and sign. Thirty-five
dollars deliver a document
for the rabbi to certify.

I think it means nothing.
Two days later, we celebrate with
family and friends, brunch, cupcakes.

Our marriage did not happen
at the Bureau but New York
State prompted it.

Weeks later, I whisper,
I was wrong. It is transformative.
The public declaration

of love, previously private,
intimate. Not the license, not
the ceremony; the state.

Julie R. Enszer

Connubial Hour

Late in the day, some family
departed, I tell her,
I am too tired. This day of
marriage exhausted me. But
she insists. She will have
sex on her wedding day.
There will be no bloodstain,
no mystery, just relaxed intimacy
of long-time lovers. Afterward,
I doze. My wife's thick vaginal
mucus dries on my hands, my nose.
Later, friends gather. Marriage
consummated, we dine on Thai
take-out with sticky, sweet sauces.

Justin Torres

In Praise of Latin Night at the Queer Club

If you're lucky, they'll play some Latin cheese, that Aventura song from 15 years ago. If you're lucky, there will be drag queens and, if so, almost certainly they will be quick, razor-sharp with their humor, giving you the kind of performances that cut and heal all at once. If you're lucky, there will be go-go boys, every shade of brown.

Maybe your Ma blessed you on the way out the door. Maybe she wrapped a plate for you in the fridge so you don't come home and mess up her kitchen with your hunger. Maybe your Tia dropped you off, gave you cab money home. Maybe you had to get a sitter. Maybe you've yet to come out to your family at all, or maybe your family kicked you out years ago. Forget it, you survived. Maybe your boo stayed home, wasn't feeling it, but is blowing up your phone with sweet texts, trying to make sure you don't stray. Maybe you're allowed to stray. Maybe you're flush, maybe you're broke as nothing, and angling your pretty face barside, hoping someone might buy you a drink. Maybe your half-Latin-ass doesn't even speak Spanish; maybe you barely speak English. Maybe you're undocumented.

Outside, there's a world that politicizes every aspect of your identity. There are preachers, of multiple faiths, mostly self-identified Christians, condemning you to hell. Outside, they call you an abomination. Outside, there is a news media that acts as if there are two sides to a debate over trans people using public bathrooms. Outside, there is a presidential candidate who has built a platform on erecting a wall between the United States and Mexico — and not only do people believe that crap is possible, they believe it is necessary. Outside, Puerto Rico is still a colony, being allowed to drown in debt, to suffer, without the right to file for bankruptcy, to protect itself. Outside, there are more than 100 bills targeting you, your choices, your people, pending in various states.

You have known violence. You have known violence. You are queer and you are brown and you have known violence. You have known a masculinity, a machismo, stupid with its own fragility. You learned basic queer safety, you have learned to scan, casually, quickly, before any public display of affection.

Outside, the world can be murderous to you and your kind. Lord knows.

But inside, it is loud and sexy and on. If you're lucky, it's a mixed crowd, muscle Marys and bois and femme fags and butch dykes and genderqueers. If you're lucky, no one is wearing much clothing, and the dance floor is full. If you're lucky, they're playing reggaeton, salsa, and you can move.

People talk about liberation as if it's some kind of permanent state, as if you get liberated and that's it, you get some rights and that's it, you get some acknowledgment and that's it, happy now? But you're going back down into the muck of it every day; this world constricts. You know what the opposite of Latin Night at the Queer Club is? Another Day in Straight White America. So when you walk into the club, if you're lucky, it feels expansive. "Safe space" is a cliche, overused and exhausted in our discourse, but the fact remains that a sense of safety transforms the body, transforms the spirit. So many of us walk through the world without it. So when you walk through the door and it's a salsa beat, and brown bodies, queer bodies, all writhing in some fake smoke and strobing lights, no matter how cool, how detached, how over-it you think you are, Latin Night at the Queer Club breaks your cool. You can't help but smile, this is for you, for us.

Outside, tomorrow, hangovers, regrets, the grind. Outside, tomorrow, the struggle to effect change. But inside, tonight, none of that matters. Inside, tonight, the only imperative is to love. Lap the bar, out for a smoke, back inside, the ammonia and sweat and the floor slightly tacky, another drink, the imperative is to get loose, get down, find religion, lose it, find your hips locked into another's, break, dance on your own for a while — but you didn't come here to be a nun — find your lips pressed against another's, break, find your friends, dance. The only imperative is to be transformed, transfigured in the disco light. To lighten, loosen, see yourself reflected in the beauty of others. You didn't come here to be a martyr, you came to live, papi. To live, mamacita. To live, hijos. To live, mariposas.

The media will spin the conversation away from homegrown homophobic terrorism to a general United States vs. Islamist narrative. Mendacious, audacious politicians — Republicans who vote against queer rights, against gun control — will seize on this massacre, twist it for support of their agendas.

But for a moment, I want to talk about the sacredness of Latin Night at the Queer Club. Amid all the noise, I want to close my eyes and see you all there, dancing, inviolable, free.

—*Washington Post, June 13, 2016*

Kevin Simmonds

Toll

She astonishes us with his head
brought down hard against the floor

Fuck with me a-
gain and I will
Kill you

Eyes mother-wide in instruction

Everyone in the subway car now apprehends the voice
weightier than her frame

But I'd already watched her enter
a dare of enchantment or nonchalance
until this man released

What the fuck are you

into the quiet formality of the car

A preamble she's heard many times before
in English   in Spanish
from the potbellied   the teenaged   the blacks who speak readily
and indignantly of her unbelonging to them

His not-question a challenge we brace for
holding the poles
adjusting our backpacks
eyeing each other to see if we've assessed correctly

as she slides her phone into her back pocket
deciphering what the hands must do if the body would just launch

uncaring and cloudless into the affliction
pinning it with her knees
its long siren of repulsed faces flashing
in this one now-terrified face

of all-seeing men   always men
or angry angling women and family   always family
who stood guard against her lips and eyeshadow
tank tops and skirts encircling her runner's legs veined
and formidable
her conditioning and theirs
and marking her evermore

Her bloom   if it is to be
must push up through the hardness of stares
thickets of knucklebones impaling everyday
with the certainty of a prophet

The ride is long to the next stop
She's on her hands and knees a supplicant chosen
to hound this evil
bark it back so this man feels
her mercy

Kevin Simmonds

Sermon

It's too simple for most. Our cellular bodies are prosthetic to spirit, irrefutable elision of god and monster, wing and hangnail.

We are four-limbed embers.

Mostly it's recovery. Take the cliché of a child whose need for an absent father unearths an appetite for damage. This is the beginning of the gospel.

Before he had hair on his balls, he'd pled for deliverance. Some clapboard apostle shouted the demon names of what afflicts while that boy coughed into brown paper bags to expel his homosexuality. He retched until his stomach and sides ached.

The prayer should not always begin *Our Father*.

Not every two bodies will create children. It's not that they are without string, key or hammer. Some are woodwinds, their music of erotic conclusions. Let the breath pass through them. You do not control the wind.

The body doesn't know religion but begins its every motion as a god.

Kevin Simmonds

Salvation

Leather boots
two polished exclamations
that he belongs wherever he is
I squint for other memories
of the tall state trooper
whose silence I always matched
But this fills the frame

I raise my father
through leather
ascend tightening bootstraps
summon his silence
through a head harness
a mouth gag pulled tight
hoist a man's whimpers
as sails

Believe me   I know what to console
what to injure and speak holy

Tell me you've never looked at Jesus hanging there
the way you look at any man
before you caught yourself and averted your eyes
from the blunt brutal evidence
that salvation is only possible
when your god is hungry
then fed

Kevin Simmonds

Apparition

Uncle Lyle appears Saturday night
eyes downcast but severe
with liner & mascara

diminutive crimson lip
black weave gathered into the cowries
of the comb

He lifts his sleeved hand
covers the button of his mouth
& giggles

This motherfucker / has come / as geisha

Dead 20 years
he materializes as my fairy
drag mother beseeching me from platform *geta*

from belted cadence of silk
brocade & satin weave
kimono a la McQueen

He cannot speak
just gestures *Kevin*
ring the bell of your body

I stare from the sofa
where I've been collecting lines all day
then casting them

He had no heyday
He hid all his life
Momma told me so

I remember his immaculate apartment
I remember his limp-wristed voice
I remember fearing I'd turn out like him

Uncle Lyle begins walking
the heretofore unacknowledged runway
of my living room

I'm a bad bad student
I'm peanut butter & jelly
He's giving me filet mignon & black napkins

I have no quarrel with the dead
only the living
only the siege of ordinary time

Uncle Lyle went to Catholic school
& was an altar boy like me
But the priests must've grazed on him

Maybe that's what went wrong in me
I wasn't chosen as he was
I didn't need to know my name

I'd always known it
but no one called me by it
& I was ashamed

L. Lamar Wilson

I Can't Help It

I talk too much. I cannot tell a liar
from a preacher, so I tell you
what you want: I'm saved & sick
of this world, safe in God's arms. God,
give me this world in an honest man's
arms. An ego is hard to stroke. Or easy if
you know how to quiet it, let a man feel
his burn in your throat. I talk too much.
I'm sorry I'm not sorry enough. I'll dance
all over you. O liar. Preacher. Daddy-
o, your tongue lashing is never hard
or fast enough. When you lie still,
stroking your chalice, the quiet makes me
retch. I am a lone dandelion in a field,
waiting. Come. Blow me to bits.   Still.
You'll die this way, saved by the lies
that burn like the ice water & alcohol
Mama sits me in to break the fevers
our silences brought. I'll die thrashing,
telling any body all my secrets.

L. Lamar Wilson

Resurrection Sunday

A man holds his penis in his mouth.
Sprawled on a cheap sofa like the one
that holds my bare backside, he stares blankly

through the lens at the director for his cues,
through me reaching for his gaze. I'm twentysomething
& home alone. I'm so there. I'm so not there

or here alone. See the boy in overalls: cross-legged
& wedged in the corner between two walls
of books. He stares as Claude Neal's limp tongue

holds his own limpness on the fading page
of one dusty tome, Claude's sockets fixed
on some constellation the boy wishes

he could decipher. Claude's body — chiseled
& mangled — hangs in an oak by a rope. There is nothing
in this body we can desire, & we want.

We want a body, not mangled like ours,
we can love without shame. The boy feels
so small in his body, its scars that beckon

stares & gasps. I am he, doubled in size
& solemnity. I churn. I am an ocean
of want. This video's hustler must do.

His left pec brandishes a lion's paw
& skull-&-bones. A broken heart heaves outside
his right. With each kiss, our heads swell.

He'll make $250 for this trick, $150 more
than he'd earn trading others in parked cars
on a street corner where no trees will grow

all these miles from us. This director promises
he's stardust, has the blow to get him to the edge
& may actually finish him. He tells him,

tells me, what to do next, moans Big.
Black. Cock. I obey. I swell more still
& remember I should be studying

what Nietzsche says God isn't. I am
at a black university. God always
enters the classroom here,

& this philosophy professor, a newly converted
agnostic, will prove her theories. But
this video's lessons will pay off sooner

& take me & this boy closer than when
he stared at Claude, hanging, in The Anatomy
of a Lynching on that long ride home from the library,

squinting but unable to see Claude's pupils, see
if peace eclipsed terror before he died. Child,
they came from everywhere & all you could do was pray

you weren't the nigger they picked for the picnic
on the courthouse lawn, our grandmother says.
In the picture, Claude is alone, but as she speaks,

kids blur into the sepia background, ape
the grins on their parents' faces, await
their turn to prod his charred flesh.

The boy asks if Claude was a good student
like him, if she was the one who would not give
the NAACP her name when 50-cent postcards,

news of Claude's fingers & toes sold
as souvenirs, reached stands. *I told that boy*
to leave that white gal alone: the only words

breaking the silence of the rest of that ride,
the only words her brother says at home.
I told that boy to leave that white gal alone:

their script a shroud over faces suddenly
childlike, each crease around their eyes
a dog-eared page the boy can never read.

The boy wants to ask where the family
of Lola, Claude's slain lover, lives, where
his pickled prick must collect dust

on some shelf, to say *I want to study it.*
He wants to see how he'd hang,
loosed to rove in a bottle. But he is a boy.

He does not know how to speak
the unspeakable yet. I
heave. It is almost dawn now.

The courthouse towers there,
in the center of that town, & that oak,
mostly limbless, looms. Still.

Soon, its flaccid branches will shade
more brown boys, guilty or not, waiting
to learn what their next move will be. It's hard

to get anywhere without passing it, passing them,
bowed, not meeting my gaze. The hustler moans.
I gasp. I cannot take this boy, this fallen star

or his unseen master's plan where I'm coming.
I turn off the TV. I am not afraid to raise
this dead flesh, for all & no one to see, alone,

like that other hanged man the boy followed
so slavishly, to ask him what no man,
not even Daddy, can show me: Jesus,

if a man is black & his manhood is forced
into his own mouth by another man
who's as afraid of the power he holds

but is pale enough to hold the camera
or the noose, how much of a man isn't he?
Like you, O Lord, I rise with all power

in my hand, but I do not want to cross
this tempest alone. I am not that boy
anymore. I am not afraid to say

I am a man, searching for a man
whose flesh will rise, only for me,
without force, without fear. Come,

lie with me & be redeemed. See
my yoke, this flesh, broken
for you? Find here

a different kind of holy, a sacrilegion,
a sacrament for our sanctifunked
souls. Dark & darker. Still.

Lori Anderson

Hayley Mills

Oh Hayley Mills

You with your blond hair

Me with my matted dayglow orange Halloween witch wig

You with your white I wanna look like you skin

Me with my brillo pad and scouring powder baths

We are fraternal twins

When I hear

Why you always listenin to that beatles music

You talk like a white girl

I know I have transitioned

Lori Anderson

Family-Style

How can so many meals that come from the same kettle taste so different?

One helping bombards, another Bum rushes, another PTSDs the palate

A second helping Buddhas the chaos to the left of the taste buds

Hunger bursts like tiny Kool-Aid seeds in a pomegranate

With the oh-yeah knowledge that this is not indeed a "Happy Meal"

Why do I always return, sit at my place and ask, What's for dinner?

Lori Anderson

Brooklyn American

White, Black, Puerto Rican, everybody just a-freakin'
— Prince Rogers Nelson

Staring closely at my skin in the sunlight I see red then blue then green
Tredecillion sparkles
You know, 10^{42}
They shine like unlinks in a chain of drunk DNA
Inconclusive of who I am what I was and what I'm thought to be

I am Jewish (Ray's Pizza)
Puerto Rican (Ray's Pizza)
Italian (Ray's Pizza)
Irish (Ray's Pizza)

I used to be Afro-American
Black Colored Negro
Now I'm a modern dance sans interpretation

Once I was Black
But this woman said Nooooooo you're African American
Damn I wish I had home movies
Proof that I had indeed lived on the dark continent of her statement

So when no one else is around I claim my tribe out loud
I am Brooklyn American!
From Brooklyn America!
ID? Metrocard.
I have broken heart memories of the jumping off place
Like when you're on the B61 bus and you jump up suddenly and say
Yo! Yo! This is my stop!

(2015)

Megan Volpert

to the tune of "Rosalita" (Springsteen 1973)

Shed doubt now Rosie, shock her from the noose of manly chains
You know prayin' for man enough is maybe too much shame
I'm gonna pick up an acolyte, you're gonna be a hot cross bun
And together we'll make the devout ignite and make our saint's day stun
You don't have to fall for more penance Rosie and you don't have to be no son
The only mother you ever wanna heed should respect the way you've swung
Rosie's pure like none
Acolyte let your self free, try on all the hats
Hot cross bun's cooled down confronting rebirth applying new attitude in all her spats
Cops cruisin' the corner waitin' for a bust
Drama she looks like a bimbo lookin' right past us
We'll recite the Lord's Prayer circle vessels made of squares
'Cause you know we won't succumb
We ain't got forgiveness
But who on earth could shun
When Rosie's pure like none

Rosalita hump a little higher
Señorita don't spit in my fire
I don't need another lover, not for hire
Rosalita you're my stoned esquire

Stack the abbot with calla lilies, 'cause it's time that we declare
Wandering Jews will all seem silly in our world of laissez faire
We're gonna read bell hooks, smoke with crooks, get some looks
Grab the limelight, we're gonna be highlights
So Rosie come out forthright, baby come out outright
Windows are for dreamers, fire escapes for whores
Closets are for high heels, divas use the door
So use it Rosie, that's what I'm here for

Rosalita hump a little higher
Señorita don't spit in my fire
I don't need another lover, not for hire
Rosalita you're my stoned esquire

Now I know your mama she prays for me 'cause I don't have mammary glands
And I know your daddy detests Rosie cause he wants you to be a man
Papa entered your room, he beat you with a broom
I'm comin' to make a stand
I'm comin' to activate you, complicate you, I want to be your plan
Sometimes we're shook up, dismissed, but inside we'll be sunny
Olympiad, Dame Galahad
And your papa says he knows how you're making all your money
Tell him he can look askance or find his daughter in loving first glance
Because our subnormality, Rosie, just can't stave off our rain dance
My throat's not slashed and my face isn't smashed when johns have mercy
By the time we can sleep, I'm dead on my feet from walking the streets of Jersey
Hold sunlight, it's a human right 'cause Rosie we damn sure belong
And in time we'll greet that justice fight as it's foretold by our harms
I know a city of some grace in Northern California down San Francisco Bay
It's a little cliche but we can be ourselves all the way
You can hear it in your heartbeat drumming
So keep faith Rosie 'cause this is your second coming

Meredith Camel

Sexual Evolution*

"My mother said you can be a nurse but you can't be a doctor. I wanted to be a doctor because I saw how my stepfather treated my mother, how she had to ask for money when her children needed something. I never wanted to be in a position like that."

My mother said you can marry a doctor
but you can't marry a nurse. She didn't
even know there was such a thing
as a *straight* male nurse. She just assumed
they were all *homosexual.*

"The first time I ever heard of the concept was when I read *Giovanni's Room* back in the '50s. I didn't even know there was such a thing as being gay. I think they just called it *homosexual* back then. It wasn't until much later when I first heard the word *lesbian.*"

The first time I went on a field trip
with my fourth-grade teacher,
my eyes fixated on the syncopation
of her breasts with the bumps
of the bus. It wasn't until much later
when I first heard the word lesbian.
She was married with two young children.

"She was married with two young children. We were both working in a lab in Texas. Her husband got me fired from the job and threatened to get me kicked out of medical school. He drove me out of Texas."

My husband nearly got kicked out
of medical school for taking a photo

of someone sexually molesting a dog.
He drove me out of Philly with the promise
of so many common interests — and passion
that soon turned to force. Of course I was scared.

"Of course we were scared. But we had so many common interests — and the passion. We were driven by the same forces that have kept us together for 45 years."

Together for seven years, we were divided
by more than an itch — a rash
of irrational words, miscarried vows
and other things that weren't meant
to be, no matter how hard they kicked.
I saw him recently and sensed
his remorse for demanding half
the last sugar bag along with my dough.

"It's only recently that I introduce her as 'my partner of 45 years.' It took me a long time to say that."

Of course I was scared
when she proposed on the balcony
of our cabin somewhere between
Belize and Cozumel — my eyes
fixated on the breath-notes of her breasts
in moonlight silhouette.
But we had so many common interests —

and passion. It still feels
strange to introduce her as my wife.
But I love her in a way
I could never love a man. It took me
a long time to say that.

**Quoted text is from an interview with Lynn Leverett, a retired pathologist who lives in Miami with the woman she fell in love with in 1966.*

Meredith Camel

My To-Do List

(If I were a Disney Imagineer)

1. Replace animatronic cave men with real cave men inside Epcot's Spaceship Earth. Watch them freak when the tram comes through. Rotate them weekly for maximum effect.

2. Erect mushroom-shaped tents in the E.T. exhibit and advertise them as the newest Disney themed resort. Stay two nights, phone home free.

3. Impregnate the ground in Tomorrowland with magnets that spin the body's polarity, forcing guests to walk in reverse. This accurately depicts the future as a scary place filled with ass-backward ideas.

4. Install body scanners at the entry point of each country in Epcot's World Showcase. Offer guests the option of an animatronic TSA pat-down, as long as they sign a cyborg-intimacy waiver.

5. Install uranium in the walls at the Universe of Energy attraction so guests can live out the dream of being a human bulb in the Electric Light Parade.

6. Promote world peace by instituting a new diversity policy for Space Mountain. No rocket will blast off unless it contains a mixture of races, colors, genders, and sexual orientations all wrapping their legs awkwardly around each other.

7. Retrofit one elevator in select Disney resort hotels with a Tower of Terror attraction. Do not advertise this feature. Activate the ride once a month or until a guest suffers a myocardial infarction.

8. Sprinkle stem cells on the heads of all guests as they pass through the turnstiles, and tell them it's fairy dust. Watch their amazement as they grow real Mickey Mouse ears.

Meredith Camel

Tiptreeing around the Cosmos in Drag

For Alice Sheldon, 1960s-era sci-fi writer who gained fame using a male pseudonym

Alice Sheldon clopped on her pearls and teased her Lucy Ball hair space needle high before slipping out of her Easy-Bake Airstream to pimp the saucer. No, she never did see the logic of fine china, having tossed her curio keys into thin space light years ago.

Not one to fret apron-string acoustics splitting heirs between TV mom troglodons and Ape-shaped successors—she preferred quantum leaping the chasm from oddest sea to galaxy as James Tiptree, searching for "The Women Men Don't See."

She looked like Annie Lenox in a Robert Palmer video. Slick-backed hair in a sleek black suit seducing a pixie frame. Twiki told her not to do it—
Don't Buck tradition, beenie, meenie, meep
Fuck tradition!
she said, she said, he said.

And they listened.

They listened to her soprano stories cocooned in a tenor drone.
They listened with one ear cupped to the moon
tickling each other's tentacles under the table.

Nicholas Wong

Airland

For a while now my hand has been rubbing
an image of your hand. Not fun to let the real
play peekaboo with the imagined.
One of them attracts time,
which I have stopped collecting, mostly
as a way of proving this reality is a fruit.
Although maybe I am meditating, I am not
skilled to explore the space. Out
I take the digital projection globe; whatever
stars stretch around our closet, near a door
hinge imply that distance can be imitated,
as if, in the end, it was not so much
about authenticity. Accept it: an art form
has to embrace its subject. An elegy
and your death now posing for it.
Seen as a whole, your body is a multistage
rocket, but breaking apart is her protocol.
You know, buttons are confusing. So is sensing
the self subtly but persistently while feeling
out of place. In the Geffen, strips of a frayed
American flag billowed in my face like an octopus
that failed to resume its main path. I felt smalled,
then an unnamable significance in my smallness.
I felt this before, my head buried in our mattress.
A monk out of breath after trampling
on the flatness of Zen. A floor sore
from the flatulence of prayers, no longer
sane and fit for kneeling. For long the world's
biggest Buddha has been left to encounter
the world. I marked an X on its forehead,
where your spacecraft should land. These days,
people fight for the right to be forgotten.
Not me. Waiting is just another manual process.
Just a hand reaching out, sensitive to breathing.

Nicholas Wong

Intergenerational

Then father gave a few push on mama to give me manhood by giving me a
prostate.
Then he gave me gold in my natal chart and one bone to break if the year was
of fire.
Then he sold his yellow Beetle told me *yellow* a homophone of his last name
and mine.
Then because my *feet head no good* (bring bad luck) what if I delivered feet
first, head last.
Then he gave me a surface to be licked by teenage tongues then I knew it was
called skin.
Then he gave me a face I could not revert effortlessly enough to avoid
mistakes.
Then he found my prostate supplements and my needs. How much Beetle
repair cost.
Then I woke from sleep often enough with the desire to repair my bladder of
caprice.
There were nights I went back to bed and heard him open his door to do what
I just did.
A mirror regretted seeing the image I saw I wished childhood was a dead end.
I could not remember how he parented and parenthesized himself but I
decided for him.
He no ask my grades my work my life so I named his representation for him.
Let me call his representation Self Portrait as Typos then I knew I might not
be different.
At Immigration I clarified people like us had last names first and first names
last.
Then inheritance was not truly linear if I experienced what he did but
unspoken.
I gathered as many balls of socks from his cabinet then his feet were warmed
in hospital.
Then he said *please* in bed and I found requests not pleasurable to make and
remake.

Then he left his beans on the plate as if to contemplate on the history of beans.
Daylight visited him through the blinds to cream or shadow his med charts, his being.
Lei ah yea (your grandfather) he said not to make a familial reference but as a curse.
Your great grandfather's grave would have no one to sweep but bushes as barricades.
No good my lungs *lei ah yea*, he said, remember virus in cartoons always looks irregular.
Curses were the immodest form of childhood. He had used both at his own risk. Then I.
Then inheritance was circular and miracles generic in the way that they never happened.
Then he cleared his phlegm cleared his phlegm cleared his phlegm I cleared his phlegm.
He no ask about men I brought home then I no tell him I was sororal or systematically polyphagic.
Then TV said K Pop was *happy virus* and the males got pregnant in the seahorse world.
Then he lived his marine life until the ocean was an aquarium of water bloating its lungs.
Then he took his pills and I watched animal programs then representation was hierarchical.
Ugly fish accompanied by oriental music then dolphins swam in an ocean of orchestra.
Then it was *Bark*. Maybe. Then he loved aloe more and more aloe cooled his décolletage.
Then I cleared his phlegm again and again then he took my supplements. Bodies of inheritance.
Then he said why I pulled out tissues from a paper box as if from the center of him.

Nicholas Wong

When the light no longer illuminates, illustrates, or is ill, or I

When I was asked if gender trouble only happened to bisexuals or transsexuals
at night

When I skipped a talk by Judith Butler because she was a different Judith Butler

And a scholar of T-data with nice hair

When I thought her T-data were replicas of my friend's T-cell counts

When he was a friend I tried not to remember

And I remembered his family thought funeral was for family only

When his cancer cells returned like movie sequels

And the cells, like movie sequels, made things worse

When biology meets art

When one stumbles on fantasies one blames the shoes

And I find the light confusing

When it visually exacts and, meanwhile, edits ______: the world/ a mirror/
an image in both taking a while to disappear

And certain moments maim

When all I can do is expunge spumes of embarrassment like the light that shawls its jealousy of a lampshade's skin

When such skin is clothed, dusted, or washed-out

When decay always works against materiality to mimic a sign of aliveness

When I try not to understand this paradox: let there be light, then lampshade
that enclaves the sweep of light

When I dance with the light and the light is me

When we both lick and lack the body of a shade

When we want something to lean on

When we wait for our night at dawn but see all eyes are on us but ours

Nicholas Wong

I Imagine My Father Asking Me What Being ______ Is Like, While I Swipe My American Express to Pay for His Lungs' Virus I Don't Know How to Pronounce

As if the itchy *is* of my _____-ness was about
to burst. We've become penguins,
entrepreneurs of standing, waiting to hide
and fix something in my hiding.
Being _____ is like jammed with creases.
I can't straighten myself like the artificial
fabric of Uniqlo jeans. My head's spinning
like an agitator. I guess my point being,
in comparison, you're an ironing board.
Because my _____-ness can't be spoken
of like this, we should talk
about something else, though I wish
to tell you that some nights,
in retrospect, were too limbic, yet sublime.
I think _____ thoughts, play
_____ chess, walk _____ dogs.
Don't expect answers straight
like your Saturday plans. Let's not talk
about convalescence, either.
"What're anagrams?" you ask.
Up bored means *be proud*, I say.
"I'm both." You're not – I'm a removed
tooth that lacks tradition. Your pride
folded, rusted like the mouth
of a needy tap when you saw me veer
the claw crane of a UFO catcher
towards not the lightsaber from Star Wars,
but an Eeyore. Back then, I knew
you knew, as you do when you load
your stippled lungs with still-bare breaths.

I imagine you asking me why I read
Sartre. Because Sartre can't reset
us, and between us, there's no thrill
but a tradition that tells me to truckle
in wretchedness, remain beside you
like a receipt, because recovery is ultimately
a swabbing of capitalism's rear end.
"You aren't like me," you say.
True: my shadow ruffles
on your burdock-reeking torso,
and my lungs aren't the ones shadowed,
computed, invoiced, item
by item, then saved and paid
for, then turned into redeemable
mileage, mane, and deer fences
that I'd pretend feel exotic
in numerous selfies to rid the thin
rind of filial debts in my skin,
though I wish I could stop wishing
someone, years later, saying *True*,
when I say what you said, so I won't be left
to feel the being and nothingness
of being ______.

Phillip B. Williams

Do-rag

O darling, the moon did not disrobe you.
You fell asleep that way, nude
and capsized by our wine, our bump

n' grind shenanigans. Blame it
on whatever you like; my bed welcomes
whomever you decide to be: hung-

mistress, bride's bouquet, John Doe
in the alcove of my dreams. You
can quote verbatim an entire album

of Bone Thugs-N-Harmony with your ass
in the air. There's nothing
wrong with that. They mince syllables

as you call me yours. You don't
like me but still invite me to your home
when your homies aren't near

enough to hear us crash into each other
like hours. Some men have killed
their lovers because they loved them

so much in secret that the secret kept
coming out: wife gouging her husband
with suspicion, churches sneering

when an usher enters. Never mind that.
The sickle moon turns the sky into
a man's mouth slapped sideways

to keep him from spilling what no one would
understand: you call me god when it
gets good though I do not exist to you

outside this room. Be yourself or no one else
here. Your do-rag is camouflage-patterned
and stuffed into my mouth.

Phillip B. Williams

Eleggua and Eshu Ain't the Same

I'm listening to Alice Coltrane to feel Blacker than God
while I pull gray hairs out my head. One wish, two wish.
I can't stand my own body. My body can't stand itself
so my head hair spirals like rivers storming up
to the sky. My hands are ashy and Jergens don't help,
might as well use water. Might as well turn my fingers
into the rivers my sister's ex-boyfriend taught me.
The strange ways men touch each other, the codices
writing themselves in tribes. *Don't forget. You can't forget.*
What colors could I wear more dangerous
than the one I was born with, collard greens
and cigarette smoke in my clothes, Johnny Walker
strutting down my uncles' throats. When one wilds out
his brother rubs his back. *You a damn fool.* Some blues
got in the potato salad. Some "Wang Dang Doodle"
found a home in my ten-year-old hips. My body don't
give a damn about me like my mind do. Growing up,
I snapped Barbie's head from her body. I snapped
like Chaka Khan at the end of "Through the Fire."
There is rage in the chicken fried so hard
the bones edible. I suck on the marrow to blacken
my gums. Somebody pulled out the Crown Royal
bag to find a quarter and a shirt button, sewed
that shit in on the spot and gave a neighbor bus fare.
"I'm Going Down" is playing and I can't tell which
woman is singing it. Must be Rose Royce cause her sorrow
don't sound like Mary's dirge though they both got two
sets of wings sprouting from their lips. *All God's Chillun Got …*
and someone reneges at the table and we all ignore
the gunshots down the street. Our names not on
the bullets. They aim around here. Spade cut a heart
now a heart's on the table breaking hearts. When am I?

I'm sixteen and watching a friend rub the blue dye
off a boy's jeans onto her white pants, ass looking
like a spring sky. His face humiliated with lust.
Was it Aaliyah or Outkast that got her jinxing color
from cloth, coaxing a boy into manhood that faded
swiftly? *Me and you … your mama and your cou-sin too,*
sneaking us liquor on the back porch, birthday cake
and shit talk in the air, somebody back inside
raging about high school beef. Kick his ass
out the party. Let him stand by the door, be security.
Can't let everybody in the house. I'm back
with my family and my sister's playing with the dead
again, crying to the glossolalia of "Tha Crossroads."
The one white boy we had on the block got shot.
They called him Cornflake. I don't know
what year I'm in anymore. Eazy-E dead,
Tupac and Biggie still breathing. The Isley Brothers
sing "Make Me Say It Again Girl" and my sis and I sing
what we know: *Make me say—so you won't be lonely.*
The generations have conspired against me.
River in my head. I'm pulling and pulling. Somebody
in my head want out. I stopped singing in church
when the songs didn't make the dead come back.
My rage stopped working, too. The cursing in shadows,
the shadow boxing. The house so safe it wasn't
safe no more. I must've hid that part of me under
the doorstep outside. Went back to look and I was gone.

Qwo-Li Driskill

Loving Day

"Everyone get out of pulse and keep running"
Facebook post from Pulse Orlando, June 12, 2016

To staunch the bleeding
sharp and hidden
as a man
write a poem
with intent
and precision

Try to imagine
to turn
dancing
into bodies

bodies

write guns
into outlines
while stories
play dead
in the walls

Barricade
police tape
at South Orange and
West Esther

I wanted to write a poem but
stuffed a handkerchief

into my name and
the bullet hole in his back
instead

I wanted to write a poem but
the letters huddle together
for three hours
in a bathroom stall
and bleed out

I know the sharp pop

Stop turning
this poem
in the dark
right now

sparks from a barrel

Words
creep to
shell casings
clot my blood
steal
onto our televisions
whisper across
our screens
I hear Wounded Knee
Spanish names
mass shootings in US history
Indigenous and Black and

How much can our hearts carry

I'm tired of writing poems
to our dead but
cannot withstand
their tugs on my skirt
hungry little lullabies

Paper doesn't
want held
but I need
our dead
I need
our living
I need
someone
to carry them

Qwo-Li Driskill

Praise Song to Stone: For My Father

Praise sternum
cracked like mica after
truck's impact

Praise teeth in
lower jaw sheared clean as
marble rushing
down his throat

Praise ghosts watching from
behind granite graves across
the street at the Rosebud Cemetery

Praise body arched like
sandstone illuminated by
headlights as it flashes through air
before landing on the other side

Praise dust that surges
as he hits earth
scatters like crows and disappears
quick as the car's driver
into the pre-dawn
dark

Praise the crack of vertebrae as it slips
like a fault line
the schism of spine that cleaves
like feldspar
Flecks of shale that glint like witness
embedded in his side

Praise the cleavage of ribs
jagged as a saw
as they pierce through lung tissue

Praise the lungs

Praise the ghost who leans over his
body gentle as breeze through muslin curtain
shouts through gurgle of jugular *Go away. This graveyard is full.*

Praise the dead

Praise blood
slow as lava
beating from skull
onto the road's shoulder

Praise gravel
warm and full as
a mosquito

Praise the blood

Praise the quartz crystal
in the man's cell phone
who stopped his car
dialed 9-1-1
covered my father with a blanket

Praise the diamond
the size of a tear
on the wedding band of

the doctor who declared
He might live
even after the machines
confessed there was no brain activity

Praise mercy

Praise the heart of red jasper
that stopped beating
and beat again
that stopped beating
and beat again
inside the helicopter
as it buzzed over the valley

Praise diamond edge
of the scalpel as it
slices skin like silk
to fit bone back inside
right arm

Praise the bone
Praise the arm

Praise the ghosts of children
who played hopscotch
on the beige tiles of intensive care room
who laughed because of impossibility

And praise the living
Praise the living
Praise the living

This marvel of bone
revelation of marrow
awe of skin that knits
itself back together

Praise this miracle of the quick and the dead

Qwo-Li Driskill

Book of Memory

— For all victims of hate crimes, and for those of us who survive

What prayers will save us

Here at the genesis of
a terrified century
there is work to do

We construct words from
shrapnel and despair
fasten them with images of the missing
sculpt anguish into seismic rebellion

We shudder under
the weight of loss
fall to our knees before
the rubble of our dead

Look at the frantic geometries
we once named Bill, Tyra, Hattie Mae, Michelle
The jutting fractures we once named
Mother, Lover, Sister, Son

What can I offer
but these turbulent tears
my heart broken into
infinite shapes of sorrow

Write it in a book of memory
that as the powerful laugh
at our earth shattering loss
we the merciful
gather like whirlwinds of fire

embrace each other
in mourning and rage
wipe tears from each other's cheeks
and whisper
There is work to be done
We fall before the voices
left in hate's wake
and open a book of memory
to record improvisations of spirit
revolutions of flesh
our mutinous love

Here
at the genesis of a dangerous millennium
we intone names against fists and bullets

Here
before this splintered destruction
we gently open earth
gather the pieces left
to quilt a new story

As our dead watch and wait
we become
the prayers
that save us

Qwo-Li Driskill

Map of the Americas

I wish when we touch
we could transcend history in
double helixes of dark and light
on wings we build ourselves

But this land grows volcanic
with the smoldering hum of bones
All that's left
of men who watched beloveds
torn apart by rifles
Grandmothers singing back
lost families
Children who didn't live
long enough to cradle a lover
arms around waist
lips gently skimming nape
legs twined together
like a river cane basket

Sometimes I look at you
and choke back sobs knowing
you are here
because so many of my people
are not

Look: my body curled and asleep
becomes a map of the Americas

My hair
spread upon   the pillow
a landscape of ice My chest the plains
and hills of this land My spine
the continental divide
my heart drums the
rhythm of returning
buffalo herds Do you
notice the deserts
and green
mountains
on my belly's
topography
or the
way
my
hips
rise
like
ancient pyramids
My legs wrapped with the
Amazon the Andes the Pampas
the vast roads of the Incas
here are rainforests
highlands
stolen breath
trapped deep
in mine
shafts and
my feet
that reach
to touch
Antarctica

then your hands travel
across my hemispheres
know these lands
have been invaded before
and though I may quiver
from your touch
there is still a war

It is not without fear
and memories awash in blood
that I allow you to slip between
my borders
rest in the warm valleys
of my sovereign body
offer you feasts and songs
dress you in a cloak of peacock
feathers and stars
These gifts could be misconstrued
as worship
Honor mistaken for surrender

When you taste my lips
think of maize
venison
the perfection of wild strawberries

Notice the way my breath smells of cedar
my sweat flows like slow Southern rivers
and my flesh burns with history

Honor this

I walk out of genocide to touch you

Ruben Quesada

Lament

This star has been dying, God.

And if ancient seahorses and whales

could flee, they would surge into the empty sky.

Watch their tails trail into the distant future like lonely comets

their dying light haunting the darkness,

where anything is possible.

Do not be angry with us. Let us resist the painful weight

of death, the worthless ghost of this daily life.

Ruben Quesada

I said, Goodbye

You don't care that you're in an airport terminal and people are walking by. Everyone is lost in the moment. Some stare confused at your exchange. Is this a departure or the longing of arrival? For a moment you don't understand what is happening between the two of you. Your eyes begin to blur and his begin to glaze. This time he cries. He doesn't want to leave. You hold each other. How easy it would be to stay there forever. To abandon the world for as long as you both desired. You move in closer to him. Cradle his head against your neck. Feel your breath against his ear. For an instant you think he never has to leave because he's frozen there like you. You hold to each other so long because you don't want to forget what he feels like in your arms. You hold each other. You grip his body bringing his chest into you as if you could become one in order to never be apart. If you hold each other long enough you'll find the origin of love, or so you've been told. You try to remember what it feels like to have his lips pressed hard against your mouth. You don't want to forget, then you kiss. You vibrate. The warmth of his hands hold the night still. If your last breath is lost in this moment you know you've given the moment the most life you have to give.

Ruben Quesada

Two Lovers

Antelucent, we lie — your body moons against mine. Earlier,
I stoked sweat on your neck in the humming of this light.
In the dark I listen, now resigned you mumble

about the arms of a pinyon pine, say it points to a falling star
against the lost fortune of satellites. We hear the grackles crackle
above a church lot. Then headlights shine on your face,

listless lips, half-open eyes — staring out
for the occult wreckage of night to vanish from this world,
until its final moment, until you fall asleep

and get lost. Your body light like tulle carried off
by a strong current — taken from me — as I helix in the light.

sam sax

Will

the fisherman's sneakers trouble the water

he baits his hooks with homophones, cartilage, pheromones.

his hooks :   telephones, specula, seraphim

                                        an adrenal needle plunged into the heart

he lowers his line into the dark
feels something bite below the river

& pulls up boy,

after boy,
after boy,
after boy,
after boy,
after boy,
after boy,
after boy,
after boy,
after boy,
after boy,
after boy,
after boy,
after boy,
after boy,
after boy,
after boy,
after boy,
after boy,

after boy,
after boy,
after boy,
after boy,
after boy,
after boy,
after boy,

sam sax

Risk

how harrowing the paradox of latex. on one hand the paragon of intimacy, on the other a glove like a father loved more in his absence. my paramour, my minotaur, my matador flashing his red sword. dear condemnation, i have read all the commentaries *raw*, how the forbidden fruit grows less sweet the more you gorge on it. i've seen the formal debates where two gaping wounds stand behind podiums + reach into each other's mouths. discourse, its own form of pleasure. pleasure at its most broken down, a series of shapes. ethnographies bleed from the ivory tower, the tower made of animal teeth. the distance between theory + practice is a slick laceration. it's right there in the name, *unprotected*, to be laid out before the animal in him, to be defenseless + deforested. perhaps this works out better in myth:

> he pilots my body across a waterbed
> full of drowned squid. in the distance, women
> sing us toward shore.

or perhaps, it's best to end in images:

> a handful of gravel, the open ground,
> a groveling mouth, a grave half full of water
> with my body not in it yet.

sam sax

Objectophile

everyone knows about the woman who fell in love with the bridge
but no one cares how the bridge felt after.

everyone knows about the poet who leapt from the deck of a ship
but not how the boat lifted & bloated in his wake like a white infant
spread over the bed of a lake.

we leave our objects behind us. we collect our dead's leavings & listen
for their breathing in the soft mouths of gloves. we believe them.

i care too much & still have the dead boy's red sweater. i tongue
the wound. i tender this mule. i unravel quick my flesh debt.

every word an object in my dark wet house. everyone asks after
the living but no one cares how the cotton sobs in my mouth.

i am become warehouse   :   i am destroy speech.

everyone knows the poet fell from the bridge because he jumped.
no one cares there's nothing left for us but his poems

not even a simple plaque drilled into the bridge's throat reads :

> *this is where the man lived*
> *this is where the man broke*
> *this is the man*
> *this is the man stretched*
> *between two cold cities*
> *you are standing*
> *on his back.*

sam sax

Surveillance

Jumping off gw bridge sorry
— Tyler Clementi's last facebook post

it's a tragic technology — the body — the camera's aperture —
a mouth — the internet feed — undiscerning — his suicide
— a cry for help — in the forums of a pornography site —
the young man — his violin — was torn — his passion
— a cramped room — a leaden sky — a prank — a crime —
governor said, *i don't know how those two folks are going*
to sleep at night — his thirty two year old man — his music —
his eighteen years — his roommate's camera
— embarrassment never ends — no body has been recovered —
the webcam —aimed at his bed — his tragedy made him a
martyr — these are his lover's trembling hands — charged
with invasion —these are just stories — the september it
seemed every gay boy was dying — beyond words — the
camera staring out at me — convicted of spying — the body
of christ — dragged out of the hudson — the video
stream — a person by nature — the bravery of a thread —
his man didn't know tyler's last name until he read it in the
paper — his last words posted — ten minutes before
— he was dead

all text taken from news articles written after his death

Samiya Bashir

Methods of heat transfer

hooyo's healing foot holds the open front door

rugs unroll beneath keening rows

dusk lazes miles down the road

everyone is starved

a child leans into reality somewhere

another swears about lost controls

— bismillahi —

can i borrow the car

moonshine balances a scalding plate out of reach

one after another enters kissing kissing kissing

heavy lids smack wet the outside winds

Samiya Bashir

Second law

Who was warned about these things:
the neverhush, the maddening chafe
sliding down a reddened bridge, print
disappearing   disappearing?

Who was told how to brook it?
The houndstooth stench of olding.
That time just runs itself out. That
we Sisyphus ourselves to glasses,
hobble wreckage down stair
after bricky stair.

That once we leave home — its gaseous
oven — that once we walk the same slow
steps as our hide-and-seek sun that
once we face our anti-lovers' anti-gaze:
bright, open, later, now eyes smoldered
coats swept open to flash our own
scarred bellies our own hot hands
ablaze with spent matches with burnt-out
love —

Remember love?

How it loosed its jaw to our kisses?
How it unhinged us? How it tried us
like so many keys like so many rusted
locks? How it missed its target despite its
kicking? How maybe its force could kill us?

Without it what's left day after day
to trundle our legs? What's left to push
breath ragged and torn from our lungs?

Who was warned
how these solar winds would leave us
brown and bruised as apples over-
-ripe host and blowsy   seed dis-
appearing   disappearing?

Were you?

Me too.

Samiya Bashir

First law

//

Sky threatens greensky storm.

//

Teevee says: You are not the father!

//

Cross the highway in the rain.

//

Stand between the highway rain.

//

Drip olive. Drip blue. Drip to work:

//

My bank! My bank of tellers askance!

//

Throw arms wide and spin and spin and spin.

//

Spin faster. Dizzy. Faster. Dizzy. Faster. Dizzy —

//

You are *not* the father *not* the father!
You are *not* the father *not* the father!
You are *not* the father *not* the father!
You are *not* the father *not* the father!

You are *not* the father *not* the father!
You are *not* the father *not* the father!
You are *not* the father *not* the father!
You are *not* the father *not* the father!

You are *not* the father *not* the father!
You are *not* the father *not* the father!
You are *not* the father *not* the father!
You are *not* the father *not* the father!

You are *not* the father *not* the father!

You are *not* the father *not* the father!

//

Are you?

//

Piss lattes in the tree corner.

//

Throw up wingless angles. It's okay?

//

Clouds nimbus. Everybody's looking.

//

Just standing there: everybody watches the screams.

//

:: flutes : bagpipes, trumpets : bassoons, sparrows : grackles ::

//

Flip blue wide-brim outside-out like father, like —

//

Do you think your hat is on the wrong way maybe?

//

Samuel Ace

An ocean-like hush

An ocean-like hush and carpet trails light from the bathroom window just on the other side of the door I wake to quiet on the streets no deal on the corner no house of friends I sit unattached with barns opera girls and faint little buddhas I listen to the tides to currents and brakes bakers of heroic scones the tarnished burdens of socks nested in drawers my head rests under a boy exhausted from a long-gone war there he sleeps naked on a cot as the north of the mountains pours into our heads I too am exhausted from war and lie curled in his armpit I wonder about his smell his black and white lips the ocean's hush as if the distant salt of skin will heal me

Simple pansies goat-haired on the green table I hear them so faintly a tremble of peeps there's no explanation for this great shedding the cough that pushes out of my sickness there's no signature walking down the road no routine no posture of papers no grand divorce

The prayers that saved me were necessary empty of noise from anyone living they did not invite me out they did not care for my masochism nor did they know my pretense they did not darn or knit or settle debts they did not know a garden of dousers or this long heat

The airport slot machines in Las Vegas all glitter and broken sidewalks the over-the-shoulder laughter behind the weather reports minus 7 in Buffalo I'm shaking open a plastic bag underwater in my grandfather's fedora wide-awake with spirits talking in shoes a sieve of coral and little fish passing through

I beg you to stay unformed   to consider entropy on a permanent basis   but you come something out of nothing and the mansions of my house are ever cordial   they invite you close   drawing you in the low mumble of bees   the rustle of bells   a follicle of carriages   cavernous with horse breath in the snow

I find you in the winds   your legs covered in fur   I find the felt slippers that hold the shape of your feet   I find your red beard and the darker hairs on your chest   I find you in an arm   a northern gulf to a southern gulf   I find you speaking in sheets   in the scratched crystal of the watch my sister passed on to me   she said my father was wearing it when he died   I first thought the face said *ark* but the little hand stopped just there and buried the word   at the bottom it read *Himalaya*   no leather   no crystal   no *Rolex* but merely indents in the nylon band from the daily circles of his wrist   the scrapes next to his hand of push-ups and snow shovels   of books and subways

Like snows at dawn the porcelain dancers in the window stand on powder-blue bases   silvery and vigorous with possibility   some neon   some pastel   some hyper-real with acid lemon boutonnières and spats   toes an urgent Degas red   the lips on the filigreed boy a tender charcoal the smooth mound of his crotch vertiginous and sylvan dampened from sweat or a careless pee   we smell that the tights need to be changed but we wait in a room full of laborers   a long journey to come   our nights scavenged in a sleep of mortars

We sing with the trains the soldiers the graves we sing with the ash our songs rousing the barn owls and the bottom-most whales asleep in the bracken we watch them walk out of the mud without legs growling and minty

Three women bring horses three others make slings for the dense matter of broken things the golden uncertain bark the soft sands and the smells of decay we glimpse the brown promise of gardens the slow heavy journey to the edge of the sea

Whispers in the marshes the long-beaked 10 p.m. birds pass through and in those angel skins we wake with a hint of going of loss then a sending cinder a let go *hallelu* a lotus rumbling and former-bodied in the rinse of outrage we become thick around gods and grasses looking for old names in doorframes the middle roads of half-mooned cherries the hollow curves of coal in dark rummage

We drive toward the ocean not braking for the rim streams of forests and slate cliffs covered in carvings of praise we bring our boots and our cashmere but we are not coming back we do not tell anyone about the dread the persistent swimmer who sinks then breathes then sinks then breathes again reaching toward the next boat

We walk with the night-blooming the creosote the tourniquets of willows and high desert owls the feathered necklace the giving of salts my gorgeous home of cups my heart this evening a store of ranches of signs of brown syrup and lust a tarry bit of hot sidewalk cornflowers in the cracks

The lines in my eyes mean fortune the dusk leads to a pink sky in the morning to the smell of creosote after cool rains grains of brittle needles the worn stock of braille too faint to read the pregnancy of boys their caves of molting earth the bright orange garnish of last spring's salamander in the still bare woods what is to come? what tiny pause full of child hovers just there?

Not unlike the west but acting west the moon and the matte-white rocks call to us like mallow beds or the inside of an ear my idiot love of hats a barrel of rinsed plums pots of green mud between my toes I need a meal only once every few days the fields spread below in a buoyancy of grains a hat for protection a hat for collecting dues a hat for holding water

Your tooth anchored and stunning shouldered in secret dreams of temples and fields capes and antlers you lead a herd of curly-haired boys sails for shirts cups for dust a curious tea made from an ancient suit of love in gentle mouths you fall into the plush a morning call to prayer my father in a pocket blowing past my jaw

You give me a blue and white boat for a hotel and a rail line I'm told it's not a fair exchange a depreciating asset for something more solid but the boat is seaworthy and takes us from the washed-out harbor with its rising seas to the high fjords and glacial bluffs where I resist the urge to call out fortunes or finances titles in ships of grief every tree bent to signs instead I pin my suck onto your gaze and choose these four fortunate legs entwined and cradled in a green purse arenas so soft so liquid and sweet a feather necklace of buds

A nymphy dance on keyboards a night in the dirt a fairy boy in my bed your feet on the pink waters turning to moss the clear dark winters by fires a flight over the bridge for nail polish a branch from last year's storm these are my breaking hours my heart against yours traveling by sea you are wrapped in a blue scarf I think you were raised by a moose

Samuel Ace

Rain a river

June 7th 9:35:26 AM

Rain a river today your butt in the
chair a moment of suits you consider
and reason but I will leave this trail to
kiss your stubbled lip I'm stopped at
the light oh hey there's a new picture
a new frame a range of chickens in the
yard free for the buckle free for the
rake the rush the pentecost drums

Rain a river
and butts
a considered
nod in suits
dropping
frayed
at your feet
I varied
and fainted
I wanted you

he wanted
murder
he fought
at jacks
a flimsy lie
I teethed
on you
to know
that you
were mine

Samuel Ace

I have ridden into spring

May 4th 10:51:39 AM

I have ridden into spring   into the eyes
of herons   I have ridden through Texas
and the bays   into the birch   a can of
scorn   I have ridden into alligators
accusers   bankers   police   a market
of whips and kings   the coroners of dark
floods   a language of keys   I have
ridden the grief of mornings   the
sorrow of poets   the dorsal winds   the
ticks

I have ridden
the horse the same
as the turtle horse
I wake with the light
and the light bears fins
I do not want to leave
the crust of our sheets
the trail
the smell of you

I have ridden
the young horse
a triad of sympathies
more leg
than neck
I have ridden
through green tunnels
I have ridden
owls at night

Seth Pennington

Some Birthday

Two weeks out from Jessica's
finalist announcement for
a Lammy and her wife, her
counter point, counter-poet,
Nickole is an Audre Lorde finalist
for a book on the Kentucky blue south
she grew up staining her knees with; *Fanny Says*
it's called, after her mother of a grandmother.
Fanny's wit form-fits around melancholic
reporting, like L'eggs pantyhose vice-gripping
my grandma's plus-size thighs in the heat of church.
Nickole leaves me tamping my foot,
though it's not just the bass, I'm pushing
emotion into the floor so it doesn't
resurrect the awful on my face.

Saturday at their house on Beechwood celebrating
birthdays — Nickole's and mine (is
this why our closeness, kin by zodiac?)
Jessica flexing in the photo because
the lemon cake she held was incredible,
more dumbbell than dessert or maybe
it was the quote from Jean Valentine:
Blessed are they who remember that what
they now have they once longed
for — the heaviness that is happiness.

Another photo, I'm playing guitar, singing
"First Day of My Life," a song by Bright Eyes
that does what Nickole says good poetry, or
at least the poetry she loves does: it walks
that line, caught between happiness and sadness.

Jessica is holding Nickole,
who is lost on the couch to the flowers
her real mama sent then called to make sure
they would do. Pink and white. *The color*
about as great as color ever gets. James Schuyler said
that. It doesn't apply here. The color
of a poet's house is biblioteca, is books,
and theirs have found packing boxes,
the house, formerly, of a strict paleo family in Asheville.
One meat for another. Instead,
it's people drinking and floor-to-ceiling
banter making all the shadows
the room offers. I'm in the desert.

It's this dream I had after *Pelvis with Distance*,
Jessica's poems dealing with O'Keeffe and Stieglitz;
this dream I fall back into in
the stretch between song and leaving:
I'm taking the same photograph with an accordion
time and again, time, and its wheeze the only wind
in the orange air. I can't get the focus right, bending
bellows, smashing buttons and keys. Every shutter
release flashes sand into glass until my husband, Bryan, sits
next to me. The reality of pace and place, of couch
and guitar takes me back up. Later,
we realize there are only bits of Bryan in
the photos from the party: a stray arm, his hair.
Even this poem, he watches me write it over some days.
BRYAN NOT IN THE PHOTO AND NOW NOT THE POEM!!!!!!
he writes in medias res and laughs off his disappointment.

Sally Mann says photographs rob us our memory.
This explains Bryan missing, but I have him in mind
more vivid than any still, drinking pear vodka over ice,
his face out of frame and still crushing while I sing
his favorite, Ryan Adams ("Sweet Carolina"
the first song I ever played him four years ago)
and his pestering later: *I couldn't sing along*
because you changed it up again. He doesn't understand
how I change a song *for* him.
But he never has to know.

The funny thing about us blowing out our candles,
the room never went dark, but once the picture took,
the room stayed in that flash light, stayed bright-bright—
that must have been the color; Schuyler found delight.

Seth Pennington

Letterman Jacket

what I can't seem to tell you is there's so much dissonance
it's like the rift of an affair. when we married, was I still saying yes to everything
out of our love?
that I agreed to others in our bed. that I agreed to another's touch along any
inch of you.
at home I'm making pasta for you and the velvet underground is playing
poems over distortion and surf
rock. there is a rain falling harder than I've ever heard and the dog is butterflies
and panting and drinking
water like he needs a cigarette. cutting carrots, I tell you I don't need help
cooking, just relax. you turn blue
with your phone. after dinner you say you will do the washing, but fork, down
phone up and you're
blue again. I wash. again you ask, can I just do the last pan? I say yes and don't
mean it. I've washed the rest —
I'd rather experience the completeness of the moment when water becomes
concentric, vortexes until clean.
the little things. later, I write, you design. the door is open. we show our work
to each other, then bed down
with books, Sally Mann and "Kaddish," until you turn off your light and that's
the night. I don't sleep anymore,
only dream, and tonight everything is blue. behind plate glass I watch. you are
wearing my letterman jacket and nothing
else. I watch you ask if you can help, and I watch you help rows of them, all
lined and ready to have you, take you.
there is only the back of you I can see, so it's my name that disappears when
another muscle takes you, has you.

Seth Pennington & Bryan Borland

Abandon

What it must have been, these
Cyprus knees know, to believe the sun
set to mystery. Something in
these trees remembers festival days, how
when this people vanished, without
a word, time stopped. For us
eras are endless; for them, time was God: all and ever-
-ything. Marking the seasons by mounds of dirt,
bodies buried, and the gold bread of halved moons.
This is how you would survive: Do not
sweat your mechanics, only your crop:
quinoa and whitetail.

You want a place not ruined by touch,
not maladapted. Something holy and pure. This
modern sacred — its structures too strained.
The primitive and abandoned capture,
make rapture real. We watch the solstice
as children of men we don't resemble; that sun,
a great creature of fire that eats
itself down in the chest of the earth.

There are turtles here swimming about with
necks aimed, strained straight up. Two young,
three ancient remember others' muscles pulled
from shells and how they filled another's need when
their meat was eaten from their own caved space.

Tell me how your own body turns against you.
Tell me, how are you going to last?

Seth Pennington

Skinburst

for the loves, Nickole & Jessica

Together, wearing-in a sunburn will shift into warring a sunburn — this could
be a metaphor for
your matrimony; or maybe it won't. We were once told
to cleave — to cling, in its older sense — to the memory of that early love
we shared, as if forgetting were possible.
What I know now, most:
the word you will depend on, cleave
to: *banter*, dancing without any particular grace and tangling into one another,
always with such
joy — smiles in you, you could not before have shown. This, like language,
with foreign sounds
made only if explored in
infancy. This is what you are again.
An infant. Learning to speak. This
dance, this slow dance of planting
basil & tarragon in a yard rooted in
rock. Of having whole conversations
with others, and your mind wholly fixed on your love (how is she? bored,
here in this moment?).

Days will be hard, but it won't be a fault of
either of you. Pace is everything. And right
before bed, when all energy is exhausted and
to-do lists overwhelm, play that song you once heard, together. Play it now
and let your arms
wrap her waist and feel her pulse in your ear against her chest. Balter in this
moment of knee
touch & sigh slip. Let your kiss speak for you. This
is happiness — this you hold, this prayer of a woman.

Shane Allison

Busch Gardens Photo

I was so fat in this picture.
The flip-flops hurt between my toes.
I hated that yellow shirt, but loved those shorts.
Now I hate those shorts.
I've put on more weight since then.
Couldn't have been any more than fifteen in this picture.
It was so hot that day.
I don't know what kinds of flowers those were.
My thighs are huge.
I have flat feet.
Today, I would never wear open toe sandals.
My sister was so young then.
We used to be so close.
I was very protective of her.
That's a box of camera film in my hand.
There weren't any pockets on those shorts.
The buttons on that shirt were rubber.
My hair grew back.
I can't believe how fat I was. Even then.
I couldn't wear cool clothes like other teenagers.
I would have done anything for a pair of penny loafers.
I had fat arms. I hate my arms.

It was the early nineties.
This was before a bad perm took my sister's hair out.
It was before the summer vacations ended
And all the trouble began.

Shane Allison

Sleepless

I just can't sleep chile the way that boy lied to me
Chile I just can't sleep the way that boy lied to me chile
I just can't sleep the way that boy
Lied to me. Chile I can't sleep
The way that boy lied to me chile. I
Just can't sleep the way that boy lied

To me. I just can't sleep chile the way that boy lied
Chile I just can't sleep the way that boy lied to me
I just can't sleep the way that boy lied chile I
Lied to me chile. I can't sleep chile
The way that boy lied to me I can't sleep
Just can't sleep the way that boy

Chile the way that boy
The way that boy lied
Chile the way that boy lied to me. I can't sleep
I just can't sleep the way that boy lied to me
I just can't sleep the way that boy lied to me chile
I just can't sleep the way that boy lied I

The way that boy lied to me chile I
I just can't sleep the way that boy
The way that boy lied to me chile
Just can't sleep the way he lied
To me. I can't sleep chile the way that boy lied to me
I just can't sleep

Chile the way that boy lied to me. I just can't sleep
The way that boy lied to me chile I
Just can't sleep chile the way that boy lied to me
I just can't sleep the way that boy

Lied. I just can't sleep chile the way that boy lied
To me. I just can't sleep chile

The way that boy lied to me chile
I just can't sleep
The way that boy lied
To me chile. I
Just can't sleep the way that boy
Lied to me.

I just can't sleep
Chile the way that boy
Lied to me

Stacey Waite

Deadlocked

The Nebraska Board of Education
member, Maris Bentley, says
we need to protect our kids
from the harmful queer agenda.
The board itself, deadlocked,
three on three.

Maris Bentley fears
that "choose your own
bathroom" makes gender
"too loosey goosey"
like each urination
will become a choose your own
adventure—she's afraid

kids will change
their genders daily,
afraid the sexual predators
will come out of the woodwork
like dirty disobedient termites,
gnawing at the thin panel
of values she's taught

her four kids
her nine grandchildren
the thousands of students
to whom she has been
a counselor. Maris Bentley,
there's so much I want to say
but I know it will do no good.

You're deadlocked, after all,
like happened to me once
driving through Pennsylvania,
when a man's hands
were deadlocked into my throat
as I left a public restroom.
I can't read the way you want me to,
Maris Bentley. My gender is deadlocked, too,
somewhere in the space between man and woman,
my chromosomes deadlocked, hormones deadlocked,
body deadlocked, haircut deadlocked,
others like me, locked dead in their bodies,
locked dead in your language,
locked dead in their coffins,
locked
dead.

Stacey Waite

Reading Queer

It's what it would look like if a circle
Could have four sides

A young boyish girl howls at a tree
Hoping the howling will cause it to bloom

Tears shaped like dragonflies
Which fall from the lines of her words

Which are wheels
Inside a single tear

The earth is crying
Tools we misuse and misname

A basket of berries
No one has come to claim

The kettle whistling
The song of the body

Gender will not leave
Well enough alone

Stephanie Lane Sutton

Ode to Femme

today i smear wet lavender in my cupid's bow it masks
the stench of unclean men i was taught this by a witch
& to heat it over a candle once i accidentally summoned
three crows & thought of the trinity father son ghost i
often lack the power of conjuring except in poetry what i mean is i
interpret dreams recently a snake bit me while i followed
the path of my lover i thought first of antivenom a serum to cure
the symbol for invisibility the root of lavender thrives in soil
ground with bones it cannot grow in dirt alone how wonderful
how difficult how many skeletons needed to make a bloom
sometimes i want to unbutton the night hold its breasts in my mouth
tonight it is opaque as a silk blouse it was once spun thread by thread
multitudes etc there are no synonyms for the word sky likewise
the root word for lavender means to wash clean on my armpits and my legs
a growing indicates parts of my body do not obey i need to speak
to you about my lavender lipstick i think it is giving me magical powers
it sparkles when it dries my lips open/close in dialogue blinking
i mean i speak in the astral sense becoming unlarge as a singular they

Stephanie Lane Sutton

When I Think of You I See

My thirstiest storm. A broken umbrella.
Good as a bean shooter in a shootout.
Mary's little lamb ain't got shit on your sheeple.
O my prickly thistle in my side, how I nearly
remembered your two loving arms, worth two-bits.
Once you had all the chill of a cool milk pint,
Sweetheart. Lately you're a thimble of buttermilk:
lemon-twisted & soured. O my bow-legged horse,
I used to think the snowdrift you left inside my bottle
of ink was a brass drum for my heartbeat. I offered thee
my tiny custard cup & all my sugar-plums. In return,
you brewed me a hot jug of vinegar. Darling, I left
a bottle of castor-oil on your front stoop for you,
& a cure for the old shirt that ails you. I remember clearly
your red nose on a windy day. You: green as a snake.
A juiced tomato. A slice of cold ham. The scent
of stewed prunes & a stale joke. A pity, I've run
out of laughter just as you ripped your pants.

Stephen S. Mills

Inside the Outside

"I'm sure inside I'm not white ... I'm proud to be gay. I'm proud to have friends and lovers of every color. I am ashamed of my forefathers. I am not like them," — *Keith Haring*

Inside flesh. Over bone.
Blood. Not white. The dark
side of things. The inside.

You inside me. Dark.
This place. This space
between us. We cannot see.

To enter. To be an inside job:
destroyed from the inside out.
Not the same. Inside. Outside.

Outside. Inside. A gay body
inside is a body outside.
Male body. White body.

Black body. Different colors
outside and inside. Like symbols
drawn in thick black lines.

Outlined. Colored inside.
Black. Yellow. Red.
Sometimes green and blue.

Inside or outside.
Space fills with light
and dark and shapes

of different sizes.
Like you inside of me.
The space between growing

small. Space kept to ourselves
on the inside. Not ashamed
of light moving to dark.

White shrinking against black.
Not ashamed outside or inside.
Not like them of the past.

The present. The future.
We are just bodies.
Male bodies. Gay bodies.

Moving against color.
Shaded. Filled in.
Burning against the light.

The sun.
The moon.
The florescent.

To be inside the outside.
Outside the inside.
To be a lover of any color,

shape, or size. Or to be
the bold black line
outside your inside.

Stephen S. Mills

The Act of Vanishing

Remember when Judy Winslow on *Family Matters*
went upstairs and never came back —
vanished after four seasons? No explanation.
Like she fell through a black hole
in TV land or got sentenced to useless-character
purgatory. But what if I told you that she did
reappear years later as an adult film star named Crave?
Child actors are notorious for having difficult lives,
but falling out at the end of the line — porn —
seems a little unfair for Judy. Though I hate
the assumption that porn is made up of people
with no choices left in life,
because fucking for a living sounds great, but requires
a certain act of vanishing. Of becoming
someone else. A fake name. Fake other things too.
And now you have to compete
with all the amateurs who make porn with cell phones
and laptops, so even in that world,
Judy wasn't really a star. But we can't all be winners,
though we do all vanish eventually
like Judy up those stairs. And I think of my younger sister
who loved Steve Urkel. Had a doll of him
with a string that you pulled to make him say,
I've fallen and can't get up. And she'd laugh
and we'd laugh. And he wasn't even supposed to be
the star of the show, but that's how things go.
And now that doll is gone. Vanished. Sold
in a yard sale or given away to charity.
Or thrown in the trash. I don't know.
Now it's just a memory she might want to forget.
But I know there were days when it was funny.

Long before men disappointed us,
we were just kids laughing at a nerd with glasses
and a high-pitched voice who made us
never question where Judy went.

Stephen S. Mills

My Parents Talk of Sparrows

Or are they wrens? My father asks.
But my mother is sure they are sparrows —
small, brown, and white.

One's feathers are ruffled up
as if it has just been awoken
by overbearing parents

to scavenge for food from visitors
to this museum at the tip of Manhattan,
where my parents and I sit and eat lunch.

My father snaps a photo of the sparrow
closest to us with his phone,
but birds don't hold still

like sons do, which means
my father's picture is blurry.
Of course that won't stop him

from sharing it with coworkers
back in Texas where he will tell them
about the wrens (for he will forget

they were actually sparrows),
and he will say what a day
they had at the museum in Manhattan

with their son and son-in-law —
my husband. How even the birds
were happy to be there in the early

September air. But for now,
we are talking of Medieval art
and monks and herbs

while the sparrows continue
to flutter and dive as they watch
the visitors come and go —

change from one to another,
but they don't care. To them a body
is a body. A family a family.

Stephen S. Mills

Pondering Whiteface in Chinese Cinema While Rereading Frank O'Hara's "In the Movies"

What did O'Hara mean when he wrote
          like a poem written in blackface?
Is that a poem meant to offend?
          To be a stereotype?
And what did the Chinese mean
          when they powdered their faces,
wore wigs of many shades: red, blonde —
          some curly, some straight —
and donned fake noses too, big ones,
          that shined off movie screens?
Did they mean to offend?
          Or was whiteface only used
to portray Americans due to the lack
          of white actors? Unlike America
which has always been a melting pot,
          which means we have no excuse
for Mickey Rooney in *Breakfast at Tiffany's*.
          Which means the Chinese were wrong
to only portray Americans as white,
          even if it was fake white:
a movie written in whiteface.

Which makes me think of the movie
          theaters of the past —
O'Hara's theaters — where you could meet
          strangers in the glow of a projector
while doing your best to avoid
          the ushers with their flashlights,
like the ones security use at the leather bar
          to break up circle jerks —
flash, flash, break it up boys.

Frank could sit there for hours
looking for his fun. For his men in the dark,
or was it dark men?
He wrote about the exoticness
of black bodies, of his fig leaf
being removed, of being taken on a journey
to Africa, of writing a poem
in blackface, which makes me think
of everything we call "wrong"
in the world today, so quick to label.
Makes me think of people trying
to be something they aren't: actors in a movie
or men in a theater hungry
to get off on something new,
something interesting,
something unlike themselves.
To feel alive when the world
was saying you are dead, unworthy,
unnatural. And I picture them
moaning in the flickering light of a movie —
maybe one in Chinese where a man
with curly red hair and powder on his face
is doing his best impression
of an arrogant white American.

Tara Burke

Good and Holy

—for T

When I am dead please mourn
by spending too many days in bed
with our dogs and your laptop streaming
whatever you damn well please, even
those awful cop and law shows you love.
Get angry at weird things, like my stack
of dusty books I never read, the dreams
you'll have of future lovers, our rarely-used
dildos and toys. When you find yourself
the most angry-sad, reach for the tiny
vibrator in your underwear drawer,
the one you caught me using even though
I have my own, and make yourself come
until it hurts. This will be good
and holy. Normal. I'd want it this way.

When I am dead please don't let anyone
put my dead body in a casket or church
and don't let my yoga friends chant anything
I wouldn't chant or use empty phrases
like *she's gone back to the light from which*
she came, even though I've said that before.
I want so badly to be burned
Viking-style out at sea, or on some
mountain river raft, and though this
desire to become a dead body on fire
always made us laugh, please know
I meant it. I want this body naked,
covered in glitter and chicken feathers,
placed on fresh, imperfectly cut logs
tied together with scraps of string

and burst into flames.
Douse me in expensive red
wine. If you can stomach it,
I want you to be the one to shoot
the flaming arrow, striking true.

Tara Burke

The Blueberry Syrup

for Mom

On days like this
on Wednesdays
when office workers send emails
with varying camels
in varying sexual positions
with the words “Happy Hump Day”
typed over said humping —
on days like this when I’m home
at my desk most of the day and for once
thankful for the courage to not break down
and take any office job just so I can
grow up and use my degrees
a job where I may one day find myself
sending cheesy email memes
and instant messaging my desk neighbor
rolling my eyes at my other desk neighbor
who slurps his coffee every morning for an hour —
on days like this when I don’t change my sweatpants
or shower until evening
and I meander through books
and write sentences and cuddle dogs
and maybe get ready to wait tables
through the night and I haven’t yet
questioned this choice, not today —
on days like this when eleven French journalists
have been shot dead and there are hostages
and again we all wonder when we’ll be next
when another gunman with anger and fear
untethered will let loose
and we’ll look around
dumfounded like we have before
saying *I just don’t get people* —

on days like this when Assata Shakur
posts an open letter online after President Obama
announced good foreign ties with Cuba
and she explains again what went down
on the New Jersey Turnpike that day in 1973
knowing the New Jersey PD is still out for blood —
on days like this when people are still
marching for rights and reform and simple respect
and we still worry that no one knows
what a day with no marching will look like —
on days like this when my youngest dog
growls at me in her sleep
unsure if it is today or two years ago
when her first owners beat her
and left her in the backyard to fend
for and entertain herself
a mere six weeks old —
on days like this when it's all too much
and so clearly connected but everyone around me
keeps shopping, keeps shooting up —
on days like this
I like to remember
your blueberry pancakes with blueberry syrup
made each Christmas from a year of frozen blueberries
that I'd like to say came from picking together
but didn't
like most things we ate
they came from a box
saved from leftover canned berries in muffin mixes —
I like to remember home and food
and those early Christmas mornings
you showered us with more toys and games
than we would ever find time to play

and how we sat in our mountain of presents
as dad walked around huffing to hold his judgment
worried about how spoiled we were
who we might become
how he picked up our trash and smiled
when we showed him what you bought us
even though we all knew you shopped and wrapped
and wrote his name on the tag
and how after gifts you shifted to the kitchen
got to work flipping cakes on the flat skillet
pouring thawed Ziploc bags of blueberries into a sauce pot
with cornstarch and sugar
and I like to remember that you were best
when you winged it to taste
how I was only allowed to hang out if I stirred
to keep the bottom from burning
and provide thickening updates
as you burned the first few then piled a plate high
this was my favorite part about Christmas
and one of the only gifts I remember
how your blueberry syrup congealed into a thickness
I haven't seen replicated and when it was all ready
the four of us sat in front of the television
surrounded by hundreds of toys and games
and we'd all eat at least ten a piece
going back for seconds and thirds and more milk
to wash it all down —
and on days like this
when everyone is dying I wish
we were drowning our sorrows in syrup
O how I wish my lips were sticky and blue —
on days like this all I want is to eat
and say thank you.

tc tolbert

Word Problems

1. X is a filthy fucking slut. This can be proven by the wear in certain creases on X's clothes and on X's knees. X owns you. X is your daddy. X is going to hold you down and fill all your holes up with cum. X is spread out for you and wants you to take it. X is going to slap your face then beat your pussy up.

2. A tree branch, or a broom handle, or a baseball bat is inserted into the anus. X is not afraid. Sitting on the grandmother's porch, X knows the difference between Kleinian phantasy and daydream. If 72% of the time, this brings X to orgasm (a splitting euphoria in which X's voice becomes unrecognizable to itself), and 47% of the time this results in a delayed 36 hour period of intense suicidal ideation (down from 68% two years ago and 88% two years before that), when will X be loved?

3. As a child, X favored (in temperament, mannerism, and embodiment) the mother. As an adult, X is the spitting image (a bastardization of the phrase "spit and image") of the father. If miracle and mirror share the same root, who must X forgive? And who did X kill first?

4. X's body is covered with 8% psoriasis, 11% tattoos, 23% fat, and 62% hair. If X is a man, how much of his body is livable? If X is a woman, who covered her body with shame?

5. On Monday, X ate a banana with peanut butter for breakfast, a Cliff bar for lunch, and 4 pieces of fudge and 2 Reese's for dinner. On Tuesday, X hiked 10 miles and ate Greek yogurt with fresh fruit, cashews, an apple, a Cliff bar, and pasta. On Wednesday, X started the day with red velvet cake. If food addiction is twice as likely in women who experienced physical or sexual abuse before 18, is X a woman or a man?

6. X was a sister. X was touched by a family member. Now that X is no longer a sister, how likely is it (12%, 26%, 79%, or none of the above) that X was touched by a man?

7. There are only two kinds of bodies: living and non-living. If X notices the still-wet grass underneath the car, wants to brush it with a cheek, imagines not a place to hide but a space to be pressed (pulled?) across nature and machine. Who killed/didn't kill X?

8.This section has multiple parts.

X is building a body in the shape of a body. Silence is as dependable as conversation. Though the body's shape will no longer be southern, X's body in the shape of a body will always be from the south.

Question 1: Who is/isn't afraid of the shape of a body (aka a "shadow")?

Question 2: Who says the most — the body in the shape of a body or the hole in the shape of a mouth?

Given that X is white, X's body in the shape of a body will also be white. All the men in X's family own guns.

Question 3: What is the relationship between fear, race, and resources?

Question 4: Who is running?

Question 5: Why?

Question 6: What does it mean to "finish first?"

Question 7: When will white men's bodies feel safe at home?

X's body in the shape of a body is currently living in a car. The car is white and has traversed the country twice in three months. This is a choice. X's body in the shape of a body has masturbated at high speeds, shopped at gas stations late at night, and slept comfortably while parked on the side of the road. X doesn't understand this word — freedom — but prays it has nothing to do with camouflage.

Question 8: What is it that turns X's body in the shape of a body into a ghost?

9. A flower in the yard is 3-5 feet tall. Everything about its body is reaching — pink and purple petals shooting out of a collar of finger-like seed pods. To the north is a 48 year old Pine tree. To the west is a Black Walnut and to its south is an even older White Oak. X loves this game. The operators on the Healthcare Exchange all say "yes ma'am." X is not injured but believes certain words are a protection from injury. What are names: yes or no?

10. Everyone at the dinner table is eating. Sweet corn, chicken and dumplins, green beans, corn bread, and broccoli casserole. Family is code for memory. X's plate is empty but X doesn't remember tasting anything. Three questions: 1. How does this relate to the three black boys having an unarmed drunken fight

in New York? 2. If one of the signs of a concussion is memory loss, who called the cops? 3. How to expose the secret fear of white people — what if our history kills us first?

11. Church will happen today, whether X is there or not. It could be anywhere. A body will fall down and a gathering of people will reach out their hands and begin to speak a sacred language – the untranslatable smashing of syllables with tongues. The question is not, "Who will say ni****?" Grandfather, uncle, cousin, neighbor. A girl will sign "Amazing Grace" to a congregation of hearing people. We will give the open darkness of our mouths back to her. (X is here.) No one asks God, "Which body, when it falls, will be saved?" We know what we are saying — we are not saying. What is prayer, if not the heart turned loose from the mouth?

12. Gloria is a neighbor with dementia. People say she's "going down fast" but last night X shook her hand and, leaning across the bannister, X noticed she stood more casual than crowded with age. X's mother was at a table eating fried chicken and biscuits with X's stepfather. Talking about the beauty of wild turkeys, X remembered seeing at least four other neighbors at different times during the day walking Gloria's old dog. Facts are subjective. Wild turkeys are the most successful reintroduction of a species on the verge of extinction. If X is referred to as "son" when meeting Gloria, what will be X's relationship to the mother (daughter, son, friend, stranger, enemy, lover)? Yesterday, X photographed twelve different turkeys in the yard.

13. When it ate less, the woman's body was an object of sexual desire. All of the woman's bodies liked it — they liked hands. She said she didn't want to be a "bad girl" — a woman who liked feeling good. For dinner, X and the woman's body share a container of cream cheese icing. X is touched on the

inside. How many hands can fit there? If X's body came from the inside of the woman's body, how would X fill the hole if X could?

14. In downtown Chattanooga, all of the awnings, ledges, and gutters are lined with spikes. This is to keep birds from "roosting" — a word that, in this context, doesn't mean "resting" or "making a home." Southerners are too polite to say "shitting all over everything." In this way, Chattanooga is like Portland is like Tucson. Is like Minneapolis is like Denver is like Asheville. San Francisco. The city is considering above-ground power-line removal. The first rule of rhetoric is know your audience. Who doesn't love the violence of cleaning up?

15. What is the word for going out to eat with family — over and over again — frequenting places of recreation, worship, and work where "everyone is welcome" but still, every body in the vicinity is white?

16. There is a man wearing an orange vest walking down the street knocking on the doors of strangers. It is 2015. He is a carrying a paint gun and marking tree trunks blue if he believes one branch (or many) pose a threat to the above-ground power lines. He is neither killed nor shot at nor run off anyone's property although he is far away from his truck and multiple forms of identification. What is his defense this time?

17. The blue tailed lizard looks just like a Blue Tailed Lizard but the real Blue Tailed Lizard lives in Australia and X saw the blue tail when looking at a Sycamore from a porch in southeastern Tennessee. Both lizards are 4-8 inches long and can detach their blue tails whenever they are under attack. What makes a Blue Tailed Lizard real if not a blue tail? Aggression is often linguistic. Which body part is a distraction? Which body could X un-see?

18. 90% of the time the sun dries 100% of the grass before noon. It's 10am. One crow is terrorizing twelve turkeys. A Northern Cardinal disappeared into a persimmon tree. A web drawn around a Carrion Beetle hanging from the gutter on the east side of the house. What is the difference between action and activism? Who benefits from documentation? X is alive. There is a siren in the distance and at least once a day X asks to get fucked in the mouth.

19. The mother X made is disappearing. There are no coat closets big enough. For love, X would subtract X and become something else.

20. X's body is divided by language. Bannister, intuition, apology. Still. Name a body not divided by itself.

21. A bluish gray bird in Oregon continues to land in the reddening Virginia Creeper. It is mid-October and the black-purple berries are now ripe. Can a color ever not love itself? The etymology of embarrassed is to perplex or to hinder. The literal root is to bar or to block. A relationship exposed may prevent other relations. R shot Z in the face and groin multiple times. Derivations of embarrassment have been used as a legal defense since 1987. Because the bird cannot hover, cannot forestall its own linear trajectory, one only knows the word for what it is not.

22. X is 36,500 feet above sea level. X is still touching her. As though one body's insistence proves many. Proximity and protection may not be related. Is love peripheral, when what grew in X's place was disappeared? Circle one: consent is/is not an element of context.

23. If bodies like X's body have been seen, is X now visible? If histories like X's history have been told, has X survived? If chests like X's have been cut, has X been cut? If genitals like X's genitals have been touched, has X been loved? If skin like X's skin has been valued, has X been protected? If hands like X's hands have clasped a throat, has X been choked?

24. X dreams every night and remembers these dreams in the morning. The most common dream involves sex with the father. Appetite is aggressive. Worship is 1 part surrender, 2 parts control. X longs to return to sleep. It is easy to admire the one who succeeds, but who is proud to be caught reaching? A woman loves the ocean and so attaches her body to a rope.

tc tolbert

dear Melissa —

a curve billed thrasher
is cleaning its beak on the ground —
we are closer now than ever — sitting
in shadow — I never want to scare
anyone — not really — I have a friend
who loves people who come out
suddenly — in the dark —
pleasure
is the same distance as pain from here —
that's my skin on your sweater — both hands
stripped now — I know I am someone
to you I am entirely — practicing
Spanish on the computer — gesturing to
the neighbor instead of speaking —
to sharpen
the body is never an accident — someone
I know I am not — letters are inseparable
from loss — moving what can be still
moved — one is sweeping the mouth —
what ever isn't skin — take it off —

Valerie Wetlaufer

Solitary Vice

I loved a girl
when I was a girl,

before I knew desire
could be used against me.

I so wanted to be relevant.
Simple exchange —

bouquets of wheat.
My dirt-stained hands,

tangled hair. I never
could be prim,

in apple-pie order.
I dropped all the eggs,

licking their smear
off my hands;

wrinkled her ribbons
into my pocket,

tore pages from her books,
all for the sake

of the lonely hour.

Valerie Wetlaufer

Insomnia with Solomon

My mother calls. I should get a flu shot.
I should brush my hair & start saving
more money. I should tell who my soul
loveth & why I am called the fastest
among women. The neighbor's dog
continues to bark all night. I should use
CFL bulbs, stop eating red meat, take
the train to work more often. I should
call the keeper of my vineyards & ask,
red or white with edamame? I should
adorn my neck with chains of gold, let
my lover lie all night betwixt my breasts.
But she snores! I should vacuum, take
the trash to the chute, get my car washed,
have my eggs harvested, find a sperm
donor, because the sun hath looked upon
me & mine own vineyard I haven't kept.
The book I left at the office, was it under
a stack of papers, or had it fallen to the floor?
Why did I forget the book I forgot? Is it
worth fighting football traffic on Saturday
to read the venerated essay on why I should
never end a line in a poem on the word the?

I should not stir up nor awake my love
til she please. Lord knows she works hard
for the money while I pet the cat & google
sperm donors. The tender grape gives a good
smell. But the little foxes spoil the vines.
I should pay more attention to fertility,
the importance of female orgasm in conception,
how analogous heterosexual positions are
to lesbian ones. By night on my bed, I sought
sleep. I sought him, but I found him not.
If every man hath his sword upon his thigh,
where should a lesbian keep her sword?
We keep ours in the bedside table drawer.
I should unload the dishwasher tomorrow,
buy birdseed & breed. I should stop gazing
at houses I cannot afford, houses with fountains
of gardens & a well of living waters. I wish
my lover would blow upon my garden more.
This blanket is too light for the growing chill;
I should find the down quilt in the basement.
I should wash these sheets tomorrow, fold last
week's laundry. I should really get some sleep.
I should spend more time calling my mother.

Valerie Wetlaufer

One day I laid down the bruise of you

In those five-inch stilettos,
she thought you were fierce.
You wanted to patent-leather wound.

But I was watching the entire time.

Rubber suit, leather crotch, paper cut
lucky dragon, loose buttons, dirty feet.

If this is the nadir, my wrist is already broken;
hit me with everything —
slanted wigs, rotten fruit, shattered glass.

But no more on my knees at the keyhole.
No smeared-lip vendetta. Your nomad cunt
keeps coming back, but the locks have frozen,
the whip gone missing.

Once I sat alone in a velvet theater.
I imagined you inside me.
That was enough.
Tiny fist curled, like a bird:
wings beating in the nest.

A pocketful of feathers.

Most accidents happen close to home.

Valerie Wetlaufer

Pastoral

Desperate men do not make patient women.
This town, these years, always living on the edge of something.

Disease, drought, revival, recession.
The woods are musky, dark, but give way softly to water.

Fish and stags float when shot dead.

One year there was no rain; the next, rivers overflowed.

Not a hell mouth or hydrophobic, but even the air here is tainted.

The ice never quite crusts over, babies are left untended, crops go missing.

My wife won't quit visiting whores.

Recall the rhyme we sang in school:

For every evil under the sun,
There is a remedy, or there is none.
If there be one, try and find it;
If there be none, never mind it.

Our hands in a circle clapped for every word;
we thought we'd smash sin like a bug.

It hid inside us, coiled, knowing someday we'd stray.

But who's to say which sin is ours?
Each time I read your letters, I see things differently.

Why shouldn't scripture be the same?

Grass caught in our teeth as we laughed, rolling down the hills like barrels,
the curves of each mound forgiving but spoken for.

There is no remedy for us —

I can't say it's never lonely in Queer America.

And the punishments for visibility are real and terrible.

But we have always been everywhere.

Bearing the burden and responsibility of scarcity,

we have long been so beautiful in each other's gaze.

I still thrill at your touch; I still feel the shock

of fear when your fingers meet mine in public.

If we are alone, it is the loneliness of crowds.

Contributors' Notes

Aaron Smith is the author of three books of poetry published by the Pitt Poetry Series: *Primer, Appetite*, and *Blue on Blue Ground*, winner of the Agnes Lynch Starrett Poetry Prize. A three-time finalist for the Lambda Literary Award, he is associate professor in creative writing at Lesley University in Cambridge, Massachusetts.

Bryan Borland is publisher of Sibling Rivalry Press, founding editor of *Assaracus: A Journal of Gay Poetry*, and author of *My Life as Adam*, *Less Fortunate Pirates*, and *DIG*. He is a Lambda Literary Fellow in Poetry and a winner of the 2016 Lambda Literary Judith A. Markowitz Emerging Writer Award.

Caridad Moro-Gronlier is the author of *Visionware*, published by Finishing Line Press as part of its New Women's Voices Series. She is the recipient of an Elizabeth George Foundation Grant and a Florida Individual Artist Fellowship. Her work has appeared in *Bridges To/From Cuba, The Antioch Review, The Tishman Review, Cossack Review, Moon City Review, Damfino Review, The Collapsar, Notre Dame Review, Queen's Mob, This Assignment Is So Gay: LGBTIQ Poets on the Art of Teaching, The Lavender Review* and others. She is the Editor-In-Chief of *The Orange Island Review*. She resides in Miami, FL with her wife and son.

Cathleen Chambless is from Miami, Florida. She graduated with her MFA in poetry from FIU. She is also a visual artist and activist. She facilitates popular education based anti-oppression workshops with Miami's grassroots organization, Seed 305. Her work has appeared in *The Electronic Encyclopedia of Experimental Literature, Fjords, Grief Diaries, Jai-Alai, Literary Orphans*, and *Storm Cycle* 2014 & 2015. She co-authors a queer/feminist zine called *Phallacies. Nec(Romantic)*, her first book, is out from Gorilla Press.

Celeste Gainey is the author of the full-length poetry collection, *the GAFFER* (Arktoi Books/Red Hen Press, 2015), and the chapbook *In the land of speculation & seismography* (Seven Kitchens Press, 2011), runner-up for the 2010 Robin Becker Prize. The first woman to be admitted to the International Alliance of Theatrical Stage Employees (IATSE) as a gaffer, she has spent many years working with light in film and architecture. www.celestegainey.com

Cheryl Clarke is the author of five books of poetry, *Narratives: poems in the tradition of black women* (1982; digitized, 2014); *Living as a Lesbian* (1986/2014),

Humid Pitch (1989), *Experimental Love* (1993), and *The Days of Good Looks: Prose and Poetry 1980-2005* (2006). Her fifth book of poetry, *By My Precise Haircut* (2016), is now available from The Word Works Press. Her writing has appeared in many black and lesbian feminist publications, among them the iconic *This Bridge Called My Back: Writings by Radical Women of Color* (eds. Anzaldua and Moraga, 1982) and *Home Girls: A Black Feminist Anthology* (ed. Smith, 1984).

Ching-In Chen is author of *The Heart's Traffic* and *recombinant* as well as co-editor of *The Revolution Starts at Home: Confronting Intimate Violence Within Activist Communities.* A Kundiman, Lambda, Callaloo and The Watering Hole Fellow, they are part of Macondo and Voices of Our Nations Arts Foundation writing communities. Their work has appeared in *The Best American Experimental Writing, The &NOW Awards 3: The Best Innovative Writing*, and *Troubling the Line: Trans and Genderqueer Poetry and Poetics.* They are senior editor of *The Conversant,* poetry editor of *Texas Review* and currently teach creative writing at Sam Houston State University — www.chinginchen.com

cin salach is pretty tickled to be in this anthology and has great gratitude for everyone who helps anyone get the "news from poems." Poet of page and stage, cin has collaborated with musicians, video artists, photographers, and most recently, healers and chefs, for over 30 years. A member of the first National Slam team, she has been widely published in journals and anthologies, and was an Emmy nominee for voice-over and on-screen narration of the PBS documentary, "From Schoolboy to Showgirl." Her belief that poetry can change lives has led her to create her business, poemgrown, helping people mark the most important occasions in their lives with poetry.

(Cobalt) Thalo Kersey was a poet, painter, tattoo artist, and humorist. She illustrated several books co-authored by Denise Duhamel and Maureen Seaton, including *Oyl, Little Novels,* and *Caprice.* She died on April 3, 2017.

Collin Kelley is the author of the poetry collections *Better To Travel* (2003, Poetry Atlanta Press), *Slow To Burn* (2011, Seven Kitchens Press) and *Render* (2013, Sibling Rivalry Press), which was selected by the American Library Association for its 2014 Rainbow Book List. He is also the author of The Venus Trilogy of novels – *Conquering Venus, Remain In Light* and *Leaving Paris* (Sibling Rivalry Press).

Eduardo C. Corral is the author of *Slow Lightning*, which won the 2011 Yale Series of Younger Poets competition. He's the recipient of a Whiting Writers' Award and a National Endowment for the Arts Fellowship. He'll be a Hodder Fellow at Princeton University during the 2017-2018 academic year. He's an assistant professor in the MFA program at North Carolina State University.

Elizabeth Bradfield is the author of the poetry collections *Once Removed, Approaching Ice,* and *Interpretive Work,* which won the Audre Lorde Prize. Her poems have appeared in *The New Yorker, Orion,* and many anthologies. Founder and editor-in-chief of Broadsided Press, she lives on Cape Cod, works as a naturalist locally as well as on expedition ships, and teaches creative writing at Brandeis University. — www.ebradfield.com

Ellen Bass's most recent book is *Like a Beggar* (Copper Canyon Press, 2014). She co-edited the groundbreaking *No More Masks! An Anthology of Poems by Women* and her non-fiction books include *The Courage to Heal* and *Free Your Mind*. Her poetry frequently appears in *The New Yorker, The American Poetry Review,* and many other journals. Among her awards are Fellowships from the National Endowment for the Arts and the California Arts Council, three Pushcart Prizes, and The Lambda Literary Award. She teaches in the MFA writing program at Pacific University and is a Chancellor of the Academy of American Poets.

Farah Milagros Yamini says, ¡Viva la revolución! to everything from poetry and queerdom to breathing. They are an MFA candidate in Creative Writing at FIU, an Aqua scholar with the Aqua Foundation for Lesbian, Bisexual, and Trans Women, and a sometimes yogi, sometimes dancer, sometimes thespian who is constantly scheming to queerify the South Florida literary scene.

Gem Blackthorn is a Nicaraguan-American sex columnist, poet and editor for *Queen Mob's Teahouse, Contraposition Magazine* and *Persephone's Daughters*. She advocates for mental health through her volunteer work with the Crisis Text Line. This particular poem was inspired by her experiences as a bisexual woman and by the strain that wearing multiple masks in her personal, professional and artistic lives has had on her mental health.

Gerry Gomez Pearlberg has published two volumes of poetry, the most recent of which — *Mr. Bluebird* (University of Wisconsin Press) — received the Publishing Triangle's Audre Lorde Award for Lesbian Poetry. Her first book, *Marianne Faithfull's Cigarette* (Cleis) won a Lambda Literary Award. Gerry lives in the northwestern Catskill Mountains, and spends an ever-increasing amount of time wandering in the forest, in search of …

Gregg Shapiro is the author of *Fifty Degrees* (Seven Kitchens, 2016), selected by Ching-In Chen as co-winner of the Robin Becker Chapbook Prize. Other books by Shapiro include the short story collections *How to Whistle* (Lethe Press, 2016) and *Lincoln Avenue* (Squares and Rebels Press, 2014), the chapbook *GREGG SHAPIRO:*

77 (Souvenir Spoon Press, 2012), and the poetry collection *Protection* (Gival Press, 2008). An entertainment journalist, whose interviews and reviews run in a variety of regional LGBT and mainstream publications and websites, Shapiro lives in Fort Lauderdale, Florida with his husband Rick and their dog k.d.

Holly Iglesias is the author of *Souvenirs of a Shrunken World* (Kore Press) and *Angles of Approach* (White Pine Press). Her third collection, *Sleeping Things*, is forthcoming from New Rivers Press. In addition, she has published a work of nonfiction/lyrical criticism, *Boxing Inside the Box: Women's Prose Poetry*. She has received fellowships from the National Endowment for the Arts, North Carolina Arts Council, Massachusetts Cultural Council, and the Edward Albee Foundation. She has translated the work of Cuban poets Caridad Atencio and Nicolás Padrón.

James Allen Hall's first collection of poetry, *Now You're the Enemy*, won awards from the Lambda Literary Foundation, the Texas Institute of Letters, and the Fellowship of Southern Writers. He is also the author of *I Liked You Better Before I Knew You So Well*, a collection of personal essays that won Cleveland State University Press's nonfiction award and was published in 2017. The recipient of awards from the National Endowment for the Arts, the New York Foundation of the Arts, the University of Arizona Poetry Center, and the Bread Loaf and Sewanee Writers' Conferences, he teaches at Washington College.

Jan Becker teaches a Boot Camp for Queer Writers and serves as a mentor with Reading Queer Academy. She holds an MFA at Florida International University, and has taught courses there in composition, technical writing, creative writing and poetry. Her work has appeared in *Jai-Alai* Magazine, *Colorado Review*, *Emerge*, *Brevity Poetry Review*, *Sliver of Stone*, and the *Florida Book Review*. She was the 2015-2016 Writer in Residence at the Girls' Club Collection in Fort Lauderdale, and winner of the 2015 AWP Intro Journals Award in Nonfiction. Her first book, *The Sunshine Chronicles*, was published by Jitney Books in 2016.

Jason Schneiderman is the author of three books of poems: *Primary Source* (Red Hen Press 2016), *Striking Surface* (Ashland Poetry Press 2010), and *Sublimation Point* (Four Way Books 2004). He edited the anthology *Queer: A Reader for Writers* (Oxford University Press 2016). His poetry and essays have appeared in numerous journals and anthologies, including *American Poetry Review, The Best American Poetry, Poetry London, Grand Street, The Penguin Book of the Sonnet*. He is Poetry Editor of the *Bellevue Literary Review*, and Associate Editor at *Painted Bride Quarterly*. An Associate Professor of English at the Borough of Manhattan Community College, CUNY, he lives in Brooklyn with his husband Michael Broder.

Jen Benka is the author of *A Box of Longing with Fifty Drawers* (Soft Skull) and *Pinko* (Hanging Loose Press). She currently serves as the Executive Director of the Academy of American Poets, and lives in New York City.

Jericho Brown is the recipient of a Whiting Writers' Award and fellowships from the John Simon Guggenheim Foundation, the Radcliffe Institute for Advanced Study at Harvard University, and the National Endowment for the Arts. His poems have appeared in *The New York Times*, *The New Yorker*, *The New Republic*, *Buzzfeed*, *The Pushcart Prize Anthology*, and *The Best American Poetry*. His first book, *Please* (New Issues 2008), won the American Book Award, and his second book, *The New Testament* (Copper Canyon 2014), won the Anisfield-Wolf Book Award. He is an associate professor of English and creative writing at Emory University

Jim Elledge's *Bonfire of the Sodomites,* poems about the arson of the UpStairs Lounge, a gay bar in the French Quarter, appeared in 2017, and his *The Boys of Fairy Town: Sodomites, Female Impersonators, Third-Sexers, Pansies, Queers, and Sex Morons in Chicago's First Century* is due out in 2018. He's received two Lambda Literary Awards, one for his book-length poem *A History of My Tattoo* and the other for *Who's Yer Daddy? Gay Writers Celebrate Their Mentors and Forerunners*, which he co-edited with David Groff. He lives in Middlesboro, KY and San Juan, PR.

J.V. Portela (Habana, Cuba 1989) is a poet, translator, and researcher based out of Miami, FL. He is the Editor of *Jai-Alai Magazine* and the Founding Editor of Miami-based press La Pereza's new collection of literature-in-translation; Programming Director of Reading Queer; and helps produce the O, Miami Poetry Festival. His original children's poems about native South Florida wildlife will be permanently exhibited by the Miami Frost Museum of Science as part of its Everglades ecology exhibit and eventually published as a children's book. He shares a tiny home, a lush garden and an avocado tree with his lover, four disinterested cats, and some dusty piles of books.

Joseph O. Legaspi, a Fulbright and NYFA fellow, is the author of two poetry collections from CavanKerry Press, *Threshold* and *Imago*; and two chapbooks, *Aviary, Bestiary* (Organic Weapon Arts) and *Subways* (Thrush Press). His works have appeared in *Poetry*, *New England Review*, *Orion*, *Tuesday; An Art Project*, and the Academy of American Poets' Poem-a-Day. He co-founded Kundiman (www.kundiman.org), a non-profit organization serving Asian American writers. He lives with his husband in Queens, NY.

JP Howard's debut collection, *SAY/MIRROR* (The Operating System), was a 2016 Lammy finalist. Belladonna Collaborative* published her chaplet, *bury your love poems here.* JP is featured in the 2017 Lesbian Poet Trading Card series from Headmistress Press. She was a 2016 Lambda Literary Judith A. Markowitz Emerging Writer Award winner. She has received fellowships from Cave Canem, VONA, Lambda, and Astraea. JP curates Women Writers in Bloom Poetry Salon in NY and holds a BA from Barnard College and MFA from The City College of NY. http://www.jp-howard.com/

Julie R. Enszer is the author of four poetry collections, *Avowed* (Sibling Rivalry Press, 2016), *Lilith's Demons* (A Midsummer Night's Press, 2015), *Sisterhood* (Sibling Rivalry Press, 2013), and *Handmade Love* (A Midsummer Night's Press, 2010). She is editor of *Milk & Honey: A Celebration of Jewish Lesbian Poetry* (A Midsummer Night's Press, 2011). *Milk & Honey* was a finalist for the Lambda Literary Award in Lesbian Poetry. She has her MFA and PhD from the University of Maryland. Enszer edits and publishes *Sinister Wisdom*, a multicultural lesbian literary and art journal, and is a regular book reviewer for the *The Rumpus* and *Calyx.* — www.JulieREnszer.com.

Julie Marie Wade is the author of eight collections of prose and poetry, most recently the lyric essay collection *Catechism: A Love Story* (Noctuary Press, 2016) and the poetry collection *SIX* (Red Hen Press, 2016), selected by C.D. Wright as the recipient of the 2014 AROHO/To the Lighthouse Poetry Prize. A recipient of the Lambda Literary Award for Lesbian Memoir and grants from the Kentucky Arts Council and the Barbara Deming Memorial Fund, Wade teaches in the creative writing program at Florida International University and reviews regularly for *Lambda Literary Review* and *The Rumpus.* In 2018, her first collaborative work, *The Unrhymables: Collaborations in Prose,* co-authored with Denise Duhamel, will be published by Wild Patience Books. Wade is married to Angie Griffin and lives on Hollywood Beach.

Justin Torres is author of the novel *We the Animals,* which has been translated into fifteen languages and recently adapted into a feature film. He is assistant professor of English at UCLA.

Kevin Simmonds is a poet originally from New Orleans. His books include *The Noh of Dorian Corey* ドリアン・コーリーの能, *Bend to it, Mad for Meat,* and *Collective Brightness: LGBTIQ Poets on Faith, Religion & Spirituality.* He lives in San Francisco and Tokyo.

L. Lamar Wilson is the author of *Sacrilegion* (Carolina Wren Press, 2013) and co-author of *Prime: Poetry and Conversation* (Sibling Rivalry Press, 2014), with the Phantastique Five. He's a recipient of fellowships from the Cave Canem Foundation, the Callaloo Workshops, and the Blyden and Roberta Jackson Fund at The University of North Carolina at Chapel Hill, where he's completing a doctorate in African American and multi-ethnic American poetics. Wilson, an Affrilachian Poet, teaches creative writing and African American literature at The University of Alabama.

Lori Anderson says: I'm from Brooklyn NY. I write poetry when my muse does a drive by. I like to keep things simple.

Megan Volpert writes for *PopMatters* and is the author of seven books on communication & popular culture, including two Lambda Literary Award finalists. Her most recent work is *1976* (Sibling Rivalry Press, 2016). She has been teaching high school English in Atlanta for a decade & was 2014 Teacher of the Year. She edited the American Library Association-honored anthology *This assignment is so gay: LGBTIQ Poets on the Art of Teaching.*

Meredith Camel, M.F.A., is executive director in the Office of Communications and Marketing at the University of Miami, responsible for print and digital projects, speeches, and comprehensive campaigns for schools, colleges, and administrative units throughout the University. She holds a B.A. in journalism with minors in psychology and biology from The College of New Jersey and an M.F.A. in creative writing from the University of Miami, specializing in poetry. She enjoys and excels at most sports—including cycling, tennis, golf, and skiing—but accidental bystander decapitation is possible if you hand her a Frisbee.

Nicholas Wong is the author of *Crevasse* (Kaya Press), winner of the Lambda Literary Award for Gay Poetry in 2016. A real Asian poet, he lives in Hong Kong, where he serves as a Vice President for PEN Hong Kong.

Phillip B. Williams is the author of *Thief in the Interior,* winner of the 2017 Kate Tufts Discovery award, the 2017 Whiting Award for Poetry, and the Lambda Literary Award. His poems have appeared in *The Kenyon Review, The Southern Review,* and *Poetry.* A visiting faculty member at Bennington College, he is co-editor-in-chief of the online journal *Vinyl Poetry.*

Qwo-Li Driskill is a non-citizen Cherokee Two-Spirit writer, performer, and activist. S/he is the author of *Asegi Stories: Cherokee Queer and Two-Spirit Memory* (University of Arizona: 2016) and *Walking with Ghosts: Poems* (Salt Publishing: 2005). S/he is also the co-editor of *Sovereign Erotics: A Collection of Two-Spirit Literature* (University of Arizona: 2011) and *Queer Indigenous Studies: Critical Interventions in Theory, Politics, and Literature* (University of Arizona: 2011). S/he holds a PhD in Rhetoric & Writing from Michigan State University and is an Associate Professor of Queer Studies in the Women, Gender, and Sexuality Studies Program at Oregon State University.

Ruben Quesada's writing and short films have been featured at *The American Poetry Review, Ploughshares, TriQuarterly, Southern Humanities Review*, Art Institute of Chicago, and The Poetry Foundation. He has served as Essays Editor at *The Rumpus*, Senior Editor at *Queen Mob's Teahouse*, and Content Editor at CantoMundo. Quesada has held fellowships and residencies at Lambda Literary Writers Retreat for Emerging LGBTQ Voices, Napa Valley Writers' Conference, Vermont Studio Center, Squaw Valley Community of Writers, and CantoMundo. He is invested in the creation of community infrastructure and the promotion of Latino writers at all stages of their career.

sam sax is the author of *Madness* (Penguin, 2017) winner of The National Poetry Series selected by Terrance Hayes. His second book 'Bury It' will be out on Wesleyan University Press in 2018. He's received fellowships from the National Endowment for the Arts, Lambda Literary, & The Michener Center where he served as the Editor-in-chief of *Bat City Review*. He's the two-time Bay Area Grand Slam Champion & author of four chapbooks. Winner of the 2016 Iowa Review Award, his poems are forthcoming in *American Poetry Review, Gulf Coast, Ploughshares, Poetry Magazine*, + other journals.

Samiya Bashir's books of poetry: *Field Theories, Gospel,* and *Where the Apple Falls,* and anthologies, including *Role Call: A Generational Anthology of Social & Political Black Literature & Art,* exist. Sometimes she makes poems of dirt. Sometimes zeros and ones. Sometimes variously rendered text. Sometimes light. She lives in Portland, Ore, with a magic cat who shares her obsession with trees and blackbirds and occasionally crashes her classes and poetry salons at Reed College.

Samuel Ace is a poet, sound artist, photographer and teacher. He is the author of *Normal Sex; Home in three days. Don't wash.;* and, co-authored with Maureen Seaton, *Stealth*. He is the winner of the Astraea Lesbian Writers Fund Award and the Firecracker Alternative Book Award in poetry, as well as a two-time finalist for the National Poetry Series and the Lambda Literary Award in poetry. His work has appeared in or is forthcoming from *Poetry, Fence, Posit, Vinyl, Troubling the Line: Genderqueer Poetry and Poetics, Best American Experimental Poetry* 2016 and many other anthologies and journals. Having lived and worked in the borderlands of Tucson for almost 20 years, he is currently a Visiting Lecturer in Creative Writing at Mount Holyoke College. Ace's first two books will be republished by the Belladonna* Cooperative in 2018, and a new book of poems, *Our Weather Our Sea,* is forthcoming from Black Radish Books. www.samuelace.com

Seth Pennington is Editor-in-Chief at Sibling Rivalry Press and is author of *Tertulia.* He was editor of *Assaracus* and has been honored as co-editor of *Joy Exhaustible by* the American Library Association and by the Rare Books and Special Collections Division of the Library of Congress for his editorial, layout, and design work with SRP. He lives in Little Rock, Arkansas, with his husband, Bryan Borland.

Shane Allison "will settle for being seen as a poet, novelist, anthologist, pervert, homosexualist, blogger." He is the author of the novels, *You're The One I Want* and *Harm Done* (Strebor Books). He also is the author of *Slut Machine* (Queer Mojo Press) and *I Remember* (Future Tense Books). He lives in Tallahassee.

Stacey Waite is Associate Professor of English at the University of Nebraska—Lincoln and has published four collections of poems: *Choke* (winner of the 2004 Frank O'Hara Prize), *Love Poem to Androgyny* (Main Street Rag, 2006), *the lake has no saint* (winner of the 2008 Snowbound Prize, Tupelo Press), and *Butch Geography* (Tupelo Press, 2013). Waite's poems have been published most recently in *Court Green, Pittsburgh Poetry Review* and *Black Warrior Review.* Her most recent book, on the teaching of writing, is entitled, *Teaching Queer: Radical Possibilities for Writing and Knowing* (University of Pittsburgh Press, 2017).

Stephanie Lane Sutton was born in Detroit. Currently, she is a Michener Fellow in the creative writing MFA program at the University of Miami, where she also studies interactive media. Previously, she lived in Chicago, where she was a teaching artist with After School Matters and a co-facilitator of Surviving the Mic. She is a founding co-editor of *|tap| lit mag,* a poetry editor of *Sinking City,* and a contributing blogger with *The MFA Years.* Her poems have recently been published in *Day One, Dream Pop Press, Moonsick Magazine, Arsenic Lobster,* and *FreezeRay Poetry*. Other notable publications and interactive projects can be viewed at stephanielanesutton.com.

Stephen S. Mills is the author of the Lambda Award-winning book *He Do the Gay Man in Different Voices* (Sibling Rivalry Press, 2012) and *A History of the Unmarried* (Sibling Rivalry Press, 2014). He earned his MFA from Florida State University. His work has appeared in *The Antioch Review, PANK, The New York Quarterly, The Los Angeles Review, Knockout, Assaracus, The Rumpus*, and others. He is also the winner of the 2008 Gival Press Oscar Wilde Poetry Award and the 2014 Christopher Hewitt Award for Fiction. His third poetry collection, *Not Everything Thrown Starts a Revolution,* is forthcoming in fall of 2018. He lives in New York City. www.stephensmills.com

Tara Shea Burke is a queer poet from the Blue Ridge Mountains of Virginia. She served as poetry editor and co-creator for several small literary journals, and is a guest editor and board member for *Sinister Wisdom, a Multicultural Lesbian Literature and Arts Journal.* Her chapbook *Let the Body Beg* was published in 2014, and recent poems can be found in *Adrienne, Tinderbox Poetry Journal, Minola Review, Public Pool, The Fem*, and *Whale Road Review*. She lives in Denver. www.tarasheaburke.com

tc tolbert often identifies as a trans and genderqueer feminist, collaborator, dancer, and poet but really s/he's just a human in love with humans doing human things. The author of *Gephyromania* (Ahsahta Press 2014) and 3 chapbooks, TC is also co-editor (along with Trace Peterson) of *Troubling the Line: Trans and Genderqueer Poetry and Poetics* (Nightboat Books 2013). S/he is an EMT and spends his summers leading wilderness trips for Outward Bound. TC was recently named Tucson's Poet Laureate. Gloria Anzaldúa said, *Voyager, there are no bridges, one builds them as one walks.* John Cage said, *it's lighter than you think.*

Valerie Wetlaufer is the author of the Lambda Award-winning book, *Mysterious Acts by My People* (Sibling Rivalry Press 2014), and *Call Me by My Other Name* (Sibling Rivalry Press 2016). She holds an MFA in Poetry from Florida State University and a PhD in Literature & Creative Writing from the University of Utah. She lives and teaches in Cedar Rapids, Iowa.

Acknowledgments

The editors wish to thank the poets whose work appears in *Reading Queer: Poetry in a Time of Chaos* and the publishers of the books and periodicals in which some of the poems or essays first appeared.

Aaron Smith. "Census (Jon)" originally appeared in the chapbook *Men in Groups* (Winged City, 2011) and *from Beautiful People in Dramatic Situations* originally appeared in *Columbia Poetry Review.* Reprinted by permission of the author.

Bryan Borland. "The Kitchen Table Treaty" and "The Duane Effect" originally appeared in *Dig* (Stillhouse Press, 2016). Reprinted by permission of Stillhouse Press and the author.

Caridad Moro-Gronlier. "What The White Girl Asked At Our 20th High School Reunion" originally appeared in *Antioch Review*; "Cuban-American Lexicon" originally appeared in *The Tishman Review*; "When You Go Home with the Fat Chick" originally appeared in *As/Us: Women of the World Journal*; and "At Least I Didn't Rape You" originally appeared in *The Collapsar.* Reprinted by permission of the author.

Cathleen Chambless. "Alienation," "Sugarcoated," and "[Gay Edge Revenge]" originally appeared in *Nec(Romantic)* (The Gorilla Press, 2016). Reprinted by permission of The Gorilla Press and the author.

Celeste Gainey. "rush 501," "in the days of early polyester," "more/less," "in our nation's capital," and "between takes" originally appeared in *The Gaffer* (Arktoi Books / Red Hen Press, 2015). Reprinted by permission of Red Hen Press and the author.

Cheryl Clarke. "Coterie" and "#All this for changing a lane." Printed by permission of the author.

Ching-In Chen. "[as a space to occupy] crossing the source," "hunting ancestors," "a lit ghost," and "various various" originally appeared in *recombinant* (Kelsey Street Press, 2017). Reprinted by permission of Kelsey Street Press and the author.

cin salach. "Bi Sexual," which originally appeared in *When I Was Yes* (Jackleg Press), "Why We Wander," and "Now." Printed by permission of the author.

(Cobalt) Thalo Kersey. "I Tattooed Jesus." Printed by permission of Jaeson Parsons.

Collin Kelley. "Girl Detective" and "Revenant." Printed by permission of the author.

Eduardo C. Corral. "Ceremonial" originally appeared in *Poem-A-Day*, Academy of American Poets; "Guillotine" originally appeared in *Ambit*; and "Sentence." Reprinted and printed by permission of the author.

Elizabeth Bradfield. "Dispatch from This Summer" originally appeared in *About Place;* "Regarding the Absent Heat of Your Skin on Letters I Receive While at Sea" originally appeared in *Alaska Quarterly Review;* "Learning to Swim;" and "Neko Harbor." Printed and reprinted by permission of the author.

Ellen Bass. "Taking Off the Front of the House" originally appeared in *American Poetry Review,* "The Small Country" in the *New Yorker.* Reprinted by permission of author. "God and the G-Spot" originally appeared in *Mules of Love* (BOA, 2002). Reprinted by permission of BOA and author. "Ode to Repetition" originally appeared in *Like a Beggar* (Copper Canyon Press, 2014). Reprinted by permission of Copper Canyon Press and the author.

Farah Milagros Yamini. "Thirteen Ways of Looking at My Ass" and "Speaking between My Soul and Sexy Parts." Printed by permission of the author.

Gem Blackthorn. "Dissociative Sexuality Disorder." Printed by permission of the author.

Gerry Gomez Pearlberg. "Oct09" originally appeared in *Lodestar Quarterly.* Reprinted by permission of the author.

Gregg Shapiro. "My Mother's Vanity" originally appeared in *How to Whistle* (Lethe Press, 2016). Reprinted by permission of Lethe Press and author. "How to Flirt" originally appeared in *Gargoyle 61*, reprinted by permission of the author. "Dedicated Driver" printed by permission of the author.

Holly Iglesias. "Reliquary," "The Game of Crones," "Word Bank," and "Angelus Novus." Printed by permission of the author.

James Allen Hall. "The Saw" originally appeared in *Four Way Review*; "Stock Character" (beginning "Jumped ...") originally appeared in *Pittsburgh Review*; "An American Porn Star Contemplates the Divine" originally appeared in *Tinderbox Poetry Journal*; "Irregular Plurals" originally appeared in *New England Review*. Reprinted by permission of the author. "Stock Character" (beginning "There is a pyre ..."). Printed by permission of the author.

Jan Becker. "Summer at Jesus Camp (for Donna)." Printed by permission of the author.

Jason Schneiderman. "The Buffy Sestina" and "Pornography II: The Capacity to Love" originally appeared in *Primary Source* (Red Hen Press, 2016). Reprinted by permission of Red Hen Press and the author.

Jen Benka. "Begin," originally appeared in *The Brooklyn Rail* and "For Muriel" in HOW2. Reprinted by permission of the author.

Jericho Brown. "Layover" and "A.D." Printed by permission of author. "To Be Asked for a Kiss" originally appeared in *Harriet*. Reprinted by permission of the author.

Jim Elledge. "Zigzag," "Umpire," "Hubbub," "Burlesque," and "Algebra" originally appeared in *H* (Lethe Press, 2012). Reprinted by permission of Lethe Press and the author.

José A. Villar-Portella. "a dolphin dies" and "A Life in Heels." Printed by permission of the author.

Joseph O. Legaspi. "Revelation," "Whom You Love," and "Rouge" originally appeared in *Threshold* (CavanKerry Press, 2017). Reprinted by permission of CavanKerry Press and the author.

JP Howard. "149th St., Sugar Hill, Harlem," "Mark It Up," and "i am" originally appeared in *Adrienne: A Poetry Journal of Queer Women*, Issue 1 (Sibling Rivalry Press). Reprinted by permission of author. And "A Love Letter to the Decades I Have Kissed or Notes on Turning 50," and "A Leo Loveletter to Myself." Printed by permission of the author.

Julie Marie Wade. "Portrait of Tolerance as a Picket Fence" originally appeared in *Stand Magazine,* 2011. "Shooting Pool with Anne Heche the Day After Ellen & Portia's Wedding" originally appeared in *dislocate,* 2010. "Self-Portrait in Ugly Pants" originally appeared in *Poet Lore,* 2012. "After Words" originally appeared in *MiPoesias*, 2015. Reprinted by permission of the author.

Julie R. Enszer. "Pervert," "At the New York Marriage Bureau," and "Connubial Hour" originally appeared in *Avowed*, Sibling Rivalry Press, 2016. Reprinted by permission of the author.

Justin Torres. "In Praise of Latin Night at the Queer Club" originally appeared in *The Washington Post* (June 13, 2016). Reprinted by permission of the author and The Wylie Agency.

Kevin Simmonds. "Toll" originally appeared in *The Feminist Wire,* "Sermon" and "Salvation" in *Mad for Meat* (Salmon Poetry), and "Apparition" in *The Noh of Dorian Corey* ドリアン・コーリーの能 (Galvez & Allen). Reprinted by permission of the author.

L. Lamar Wilson. "I Can't Help It" and "Resurrection Sunday" originally appeared in *Sacrilegion* (Carolina Wren Press, 2013). Reprinted by permission of the author.

Lori Anderson. "Hayley Mills," "Brooklyn American," and "Family-style." Printed by permission of the author.

Megan Volpert. "to the tune of 'Rosalita' (Springsteen 1973)." Printed by permission of the author.

Meredith Camel. "Sexual Evolution," "My To-Do List." Printed by permission of author. "Tiptreeing around the Cosmos in Drag" originally appeared in *Gertrude,* 2011. Reprinted by permission of the author.

Nicholas Wong. "Airland" originally appeared in *Third Coast*, "Intergenerational" in *Grist*, "When the light no longer illuminates, illustrates, or is ill, or I" in *Los Angeles Review*, and "I Imagine My Father Asking Me What Being _____ Is Like, While I Swipe My American Express to Pay for His Lungs' Virus I Don't Know How to Pronounce" in *Copper Nickel.* Reprinted by permission of the author.

Phillip B. Williams. "Do-rag" and "Eleggua and Eshu Ain't the Same" originally appeared in *Thief in the Interior* (Alice James Books, 2016). Reprinted by permission of Alice James Books and the author.

Qwo-Li Driskill. "Map of the Americas" and "Book of Memory" originally appeared in *Walking with Ghosts* (Salt Publishing, 2005). Reprinted by permission of Salt Publishing and the author. Praise Song for Stone" originally appeared in the online journal *Connotation Press*. "Loving Day" originally appeared in *La Bloga: Online Floricanto* and *GLQ: A Journal of Lesbian and Gay Studies.* Reprinted by permission of the author.

Ruben Quesada. "Lament," originally appeared in *Miramar,* "I Said, Goodbye" in *Public Pool*, and "Two Lovers" in *The Rumpus*. Reprinted by permission of the author.

sam sax. "Will" originally published in *The Collagist*, "Risk" in *Apogee*, "Objectophile" in *Meridian*, and "Surveillance" in *Washington Square Review.* Reprinted by permission of the author.

Samiya Bashir. "Second Law," "Methods of heat transfer, and "First Law" originally appeared in *Field Theories* (Nightboat Books, 2017). Reprinted by permission of Nightboat Books and the author.

Samuel Ace. "An ocean-like hush" originally appeared in *Posit* and "I have ridden into spring" in *Under a Warm Green Linden.* Reprinted by permission of author. "Rain a river" is printed by permission of the author.

Seth Pennington. "Some Birthday" first appeared in *Tertulia* (Sibling Rivalry Press, 2017) and is reprinted by permission of the author. "Letterman Jacket," "Abandon," and "Skinburst," are reprinted by permission of the author.

Shane Allison. "Busch Gardens Photo" originally appeared in *Nepantla*, reprinted by permission of author. "Sleepless" was previously published in *West Wind Review* and is printed by permission of the author.

Stacey Waite. "Deadlocked" and "Reading Queer." Printed by permission of the author.

Stephanie Lane Sutton. "Ode to Femme" and "When I Think of You I See." Printed by permission of the author.

Stephen S. Mills. "Inside the Outside," "The Act of Vanishing," "My Parents Talk of Sparrows," and "Pondering Whiteface in Chinese Cinema While Rereading Frank O'Hara's 'In the Movies.'" Printed by permission of the author.

Tara Burke. "Good and Holy" originally appeared in *The Fourth River*, reprinted by permission of author; and "The Blueberry Syrup," printed by permission of the author.

tc Tolbert. "Word Problems," and "dear Melissa—". Printed by permission of the author.

Valerie Wetlaufer. "Solitary Vice," "Insomnia with Solomon," and "One day I laid down the bruise of you" originally appeared in *Mysterious Acts By My People* (Sibling Rivalry Press, 2014). "Pastoral" originally appeared *in Call Me by My Other Name* (Sibling Rivalry Press, 2016). Reprinted by permission of the author.

About the Editors

Maureen Seaton has authored seventeen poetry collections, both solo and collaborative. Her awards include the Iowa Poetry Prize and the Lambda Literary Award for *Furious Cooking*, the Audre Lorde Award for *Venus Examines Her Breast,* an NEA, and two Pushcarts. Her memoir, *Sex Talks to Girls,* also garnered a "Lammy."

Seaton teaches creative writing at the University of Miami, Florida, where she first met Neil de la Flor and collaborated with him on *Sinéad O'Connor and Her Coat of a Thousand Bluebirds* (Firewheel Editions, 2011, winner of the Sentence Book Award) and with both Neil and Kristine Snodgrass on *Two Thieves and a Liar* (Jackleg Press, 2012). A new solo collection, *Fisher,* is due out from Black Lawrence Press in 2018. Follow Maureen on Twitter at @ mseaton9.

Neil de la Flor is a writer, educator, artist, and executive director of Reading Queer, a Miami-based organization dedicated to promoting and fostering queer literary culture in South Florida. His first book, *Almost Dorothy,* won the 2009 Marsh Hawk Press Poetry Prize and was published in 2010. Marsh Hawk also published his second collection, *An Elephant's Memory of Blizzards* in 2013.

Of *Sinéad O'Connor and Her Coat of a Thousand Bluebirds,* his premier collaboration with Maureen Seaton, Sarah Burghauser writes in the Lambda Literary Review: "Lusty, swanky, and well-toned, these poems are playful without being light, and smart without being esoteric. Read this book to witness an inspiring dexterity with language. Read this book for a loving sucker-punch to the brain. Read this book in a place where it is okay to lol, or even to loofah."

For more information, visit Neil de la Flor's website or follow him on Twitter @neil_delaflor.

Editors Neil de la Flor and Maureen Seaton read from *Sinéad O'Connor and Her Coat of a Thousand Bluebirds* at Acequia Booksellers, Albuquerque, New Mexico, June, 2012.